Celebrating the Silver Jubilee of King George V in a Birmingham Street, 6th May 1935.
Reproduced by permission of Birmingham Central Library
Local Studies Department.

Memories of a 'Twenties Child

by Douglas V. Jones

*A nostalgic trip into one man's childhood and youth
during the years between the wars.*

*A profusely illustrated reminder of the age of steam,
gas-lamps, crystal-sets and tramcars,
evoking the mood and atmosphere of Birmingham
and Sutton Coldfield in the 'twenties
and 'thirties.*

PUBLISHED BY

Westwood Press Publications

PRINT SHOP, 44 BOLDMERE ROAD, SUTTON COLDFIELD
WEST MIDLANDS   TELEPHONE: 021-354 5913

THE AUTHOR

Douglas V. Jones, a retired local government officer, was born at Smethwick in 1917 and moved to Sutton Coldfield with his parents in 1926. He served with the Royal Engineers throughout the Second World War and spent three years in the Middle East. For many years he was a WEA lecturer and a regular contributor to the press on local environmental issues in the West Midlands.

Since retiring in 1979 he has written several books, including *Memories of a 'Twenties Child* and, more recently, a sequel to it: *Duration Man: 1939—1946* which recounts his experiences during the war years. He is known to many Midlanders as a local historian and for his broadcasts and illustrated talks on a variety of subjects. His popular books, *The Royal Town of Sutton Coldfield: A Commemorative History* and *Sutton Park: Its History and Wildlife* have shown many people the treasures, both natural and historical, on their own doorsteps.

To Vic Cox, remembering a long friendship.

———————

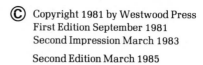 Copyright 1981 by Westwood Press
First Edition September 1981
Second Impression March 1983

Second Edition March 1985

 Printed and Published by The Westwood Press, Print Shop
44 Boldmere Road, Sutton Coldfield. Produced by photo offset text photo-typeset. Paper: 100 gsm coated Cartridge.

4

Contents

The Art Gallery, c. 1929
Photo: J. Willoughby Harrison

Christmas, 1918, only a month after the end of the bloodiest war in history, was not a time of great jubilation. But, after all the shortages of the previous four years, the prospect of a bottle of whisky was sufficient to attract this long queue outside a wine and spirits shop in Dale End.

Introduction

My own childhood and youth fits in almost perfectly to the lost world of the two inter-war decades, for I was born in 1917 and I came of age just a few weeks after Neville Chamberlain made his abortive peace with Adolf Hitler in the Autumn of 1938. This little book is a personal memoir of that era, in part history, in part autobiography, wherein I have tried to achieve the historian's goal of objectivity where the two strands have met.

Douglas V. Jones

The author in the back of the Morgan Runabout, circa 1925 — see page 12.

CHAPTER I

Memories of a 'Twenties Child

*Our lives are bursting at the seams
with petty details.*
                    Louis MacNeice

IT HAD BEEN the war to end wars, or so the jingo press described it. For four years men had been killed, maimed and mutilated on a scale hitherto unknown. Then, at the eleventh hour of the eleventh day of the eleventh month of 1918 it had ended so abruptly that, according to Winston Churchill, soldiers had stood motionless in the silence, looking at each other with vacant eyes.

In Birmingham, too, the Peace came suddenly and unexpectedly to a city whose many skills had, by the fifth year of hostilities, been diverted to the production of Mills-bombs, shells, cartridges, Lewis-guns, rifles, armoured cars, aeroplanes and other impedimenta of war. Celebrations brought thousands of people into the city. For two days Victoria Square rang to the sounds of bands, singing and speech-making. The sky at night was lit by fireworks, flares and searchlights; an illuminated tramcar toured the streets and on Barr Beacon and the Lickey Hills there were huge bonfires.

The festivities were mingled with sorrow for the dead and maimed. Church services were held all over the city. The *Birmingham Mail*, in a Victory editorial, quoted Tennyson:

Blow trumpet, the long night hath roll'd away!

I was just a year old.

For the first nine years of my life I lived in the house at Bearwood where I was born. My parents were newcomers to the Midlands, having left their native Hereford a few years earlier. During the war my father had been called up under Lord Derby's conscription scheme and had received the 'King's shilling', but because he suffered from bronchitis and was graded 'C.3', his employer had persuaded the authorities that he would be more useful at home, with the result that his military service lasted only for a day. On this account, however, I was no less aware of the spectre of war which, during my early childhood, hung like a pall of gloom over England, with people talking in bated breath of the holocaust which had, so recently, shattered the lives of untold millions. Harrowing tales of sudden death and unimaginable suffering were to be heard on all sides, and wandering bands of blinded and war-maimed ex-servicemen turned musicians played at every street corner.

I was an only child and self-sufficiency came to me early. Children were scarce among our neighbours, who were mostly elderly. When I played out-of-doors, my mother would only allow me to do so in our small garden, which I shared with a few hens, and which I chased when I thought that no-one was looking. Keeping hens had, I suppose, been a part of my parents' war effort. Eggs must have become a staple item of food with my father, for he frequently had them beaten up raw in tea. One day, to my regret, a man came round to kill the hens, which left a void in my young life. Compensation came when I discovered that the surviving hen-house made an ideal den, around which I created a fantasy world exclusively my own.

Over the fence in the next garden my frequent companion was old Albert Short, a Rabelaisian character, who made jokes of an earthy kind, such as I had not heard before. I was encouraged to call him 'Abey', presumably because it was easier than 'Albert' for a young child to get his tongue round. On Sunday evenings in summer, Abey and his wife would set out for Lightwoods Park to listen to the band, he wearing his billy-cock hat at a jaunty angle and with a rose in his buttonhole, looking prosperous beyond his station, she staid and matronly, lacking his panache. When, quite suddenly, Abey died, I was told — in accordance with the wish of his widow — that he had been taken ill and had 'gone away to get better'. But on the day of his funeral, peeping through a chink in the drawn front-room curtains, I saw the hearse outside with its glossy black, beplumed horses, and sensed for the first time the finality of death.

*　*　*　*　*

With my parents, c. 1923.

City streets in the 'twenties were still the province of the horse, despite increasing motor-traffic, and parents still warned their children before sending them on errands: "Mind the horse-road!" Both marriages and funerals were accompanied by the rhythm of horses' hooves — and births, too, in those places where the doctor still did his rounds by horse and carriage. Most tradesmen, including the baker, the butcher and the greengrocer, relied on the horse for their livelihood, and early mornings rang to the sound of churns and cans, carried by the milkman in his little horse-drawn float. There were no hermetically sealed bottles then. The milkman, standing on the step, would ladle the day's requirements into a jug, and on frosty winter mornings, fears were sometimes felt lest the dewdrop on the end of the milkman's nose should fall into the daily pint.

On the arterial roads of England, the internal combustion engine was already in the ascendency — a fact which came to my notice at the age of four. My hitherto somewhat circumscribed life took on new horizons when my father bought a motor-bike and sidecar, in which he transported my mother and me into the neighbouring countryside, and for a holiday in Weston-Super-Mare, which included a voyage by steamer across the Bristol Channel to visit our relations in Cardiff. The year was 1922, and the motor-magnates were beginning to spew their mass-produced models onto winding English roads, many of them little changed since the passing of the stage-coach, half a century earlier. Austins and 'bull-nosed' Morrises were proliferating, and a wide range of other, more expensive models were already on the market.

It was said of Herbert Austin that his wife sowed the seed of his idea for the 'Baby' Austin car. She would, when out driving with her husband on wet days, nudge him on passing whole families on motor-bikes and in sidecars, soaked to the skin, and say: "Just look at those poor souls. Can't you invent something to keep them out of the wet?" The tiny car, when first produced at Longbridge, was received with scepticism, being looked upon as little better than a toy, but by 1927, 20,000 a year were coming off the production line. It cost, originally, £165, but later fell in price to £120.

My father did not buy an Austin, but he soon graduated from a motor-cycle combination to a 'Morgan Runabout', a diminutive open, three-wheeler, cranked from the side with a starting-handle, like a clockwork toy. Leather helmeted and well wrapped up, I sat in the back with our fox-terrier, Gyp, whose safety became my responsibility. One day, to my considerable alarm, when my father was making a right-hand turn, Gyp jumped out and was dragged along the road for some distance by his lead, which was attached to the frame of the hood. "You careless little Devil!" my father snapped, stopping quickly. The dog appeared to be none the worse for his neck-stretching experience, but I was more watchful in future.

With our greater mobility, my father took up fishing, which entailed frequent visits to Holt Fleet on the Severn and, when time permitted, to Lechlade on the Thames. On one summer visit to Lechlade, due to there being no available accommodation for the night, we slept in a barn

Morgan Runabout Days c. 1925

within the cramped confines of the Morgan. Morning there brought a new delight when I awoke to the sight and sound of swallows, wheeling and twittering around their nests on the beams overhead. Our longest journey in the Morgan was to Lowestoft in the summer of 1924, where we stayed for a week. There, for the first time, I savoured the saline pleasures of exploring innumerable rock-pools in search of star-fish, whelks, winkles, sea-snails, tiny crabs and other creatures hitherto unknown to me. The experience was enhanced by having the company of Pauline, a little girl, two years my senior, who was staying at the same boarding-house as I was.

Motoring wasn't the only wonder of the age to make its impact on my young life. 'The wireless' was another which, with its weird crackling and humming, occasionally interspersed with intelligible sounds, became almost overnight a mass cult. Those sounds — intelligible and otherwise — first began to be transmitted in November, 1922 by the British Broadcasting Company — later to become the British Broadcasting Corporation. Birmingham was one of eight towns up and down the country which acquired broadcasting stations, and local transmissions were made from the G.E.C. at Witton. It was stated officially that there was no reason why anyone in the immediate locality who was solely interested in receiving the official programme should need more than a crystal-set. The necessity, however, for an outside aerial was stressed.

Manufactured wireless-sets, whether with valves or crystals, were expensive, a fact which sparked off what was described as the biggest do-it-yourself boom of all time. The man-in-the-street, working from a blueprint, made his own crystal-set, and through the medium of head-'phones, and with a little acquired skill in 'tickling the cat's whisker', he was soon receiving, however faintly and falteringly, the coveted sounds. My father was bitten early by the broadcasting bug, and having built his set, he acted on the best advice by planting a huge aerial or 'wireless pole' at the bottom of the garden, this being a preliminary to what he, no doubt, hoped would be good reception. Whether the end justified the means is doubtful, for reception — initially, at any rate — was spasmodic and unimpressive.

One prerequisite for youthful entertainment in the 'twenties was that it should be cheap, preferably free — not because of meanness, but when one's income was a penny a week, there was little scope for frivolous expenditure. In those days, of course, the 'Saturday penny' bought quite a sweet and sickly cornucopia at the corner shop, but having spent a week's pocket money within minutes of receiving it, any other cash forthcoming was in the nature of 'pennies from Heaven'. Fortunately, due to my mother's thriftiness through the year, financial restraints were usually relaxed towards Christmas-time.

She would commence her shopping sorties along Bearwood Road some weeks before the festive season in preparation for a family gathering at home. Sometimes she would take me to Birmingham on the tram, when we would visit the city stores. The multiplicity of Father Christmases, my mother explained, was more apparent than real, for those red-cloaked winter immigrants to the emporiums were charlatans, behind whose candy-flossed countenances lurked catch-penny con-men, far removed from the one and only benevolent Santa Claus who did the honours every Christmas Eve.

The approach to the great day brought a gathering excitement, culminating in the insomnic speculation after candle-snuffing on Christmas Eve over the likely contents of stocking or pillowcase, so soon to be filled with such items as brightly painted wooden soldiers; clockwork trains and motor-cars; Meccano sets; tram-conductors' outfits; Noah's arks, complete with animals; ludo, tiddleywinks, sugar-pigs and Turkish-delight.

Christmas was the time for seeing some at least of my numerous aunts and uncles. I was fond of them all in varying degrees, but it was to those of my uncles who were in some way idiosyncratic that I was particularly drawn and who became my folk-heroes. Uncle Charlie, jovial and prematurely white-haired — due, it was thought, to his searing experiences in the Great War — was always good fun, and he never gave me less than half-a-crown whenever we met, which in those days was in itself idiosyncratic. He also gave a lurid account of his war experiences, with a salty commentary on our allies, the French, whom he disliked, and our enemies, the Germans, whom he disliked somewhat less.

I had two uncles named Tom: one of them lived just along the road from my home, the other owned an outfitter's shop in Cirencester. Uncle Tom No. 1 was of a serious turn of mind, with a sepulchral voice to match, which gave him all the gravity of a Roman senator, or an English bishop. Uncle Tom No. 2 was a quietly-spoken, tremulous man, who always seemed on the point of having a nervous breakdown, but never actually did. His nervousness assumed a new significance when he bought a rather splendid Felix touring-car which, because of his tremulous state, he was unable to drive, and the task of doing so consequently devolved on one or other of his older children.

Uncle Jack was one of my father's brothers. He had been a prisoner-of-war in Germany and told of having seen starving Russian prisoners standing on their heads in the swill-bins in the prison compounds and of other prisoners rubbing minor sores on their bodies with their filthy tunics so as to inflame them in the hope of getting into the sick-bay and so receiving better food. When he was repatriated and demobbed, he was unable to find work, so signed on again for a tour of duty with the army in India. I remember his return from there when, getting up one cold winter's morning, I saw him lying on the rug in front of the fire. He had arrived at our home from his port of disembarkation in the middle of the night, and had slept by the hearth for the warmth. He, too, had a fund of stories, and because the war had not lessened his natural ebullience and good humour, his were all droll rather than harrowing tales, in which he often managed to cock a snook at the system and, in an oblique way, revealed the pomposity of those who enjoyed a little brief authority in war-time.

Following his return from India, Uncle Jack acquired, within the shortest possible time, a wife and daughter, and was only in England briefly before coming to the conclusion that the bleak economic climate here was not for him. He and another of my father's brothers, Len — the quiet one of the family — emigrated to Australia, and the last I ever saw of them was when my mother took me one afternoon to Snow Hill Station — that wonderful temple dedicated to the power and majesty of steam — where, through a railway-carriage window, we had a few words with them. They were on their way from London to Liverpool, their port of embarkation. Uncle Jack's young wife and daughter followed him out at a later date, and none of them returned to England again.

My father's youngest brother, Harold, never really seemed like an uncle at all, for he was only a few years my senior. My earliest recollection of him was as a boy of about twelve who came to stay at my home. He grew into a tall, rather aloof young man, who turned to religion at an early age. But he was not without quiet humour, and although I usually addressed him as 'Hal', I would sometimes call him 'Uncle' when I wanted to provoke him into some sort of verbal exchange. He won my youthful respect by his considerable knowledge of wild birds, and I admired his particular brand of 'muscular Christianity', which he demonstrated by his ability to climb trees in his quest for birds' nests.

Uncle Jim was the second husband of my mother's eldest sister. He had that rare indefinable quality which enabled him to meet a small boy on equal terms without a trace of condescension. He would turn his hand to almost any game or boyish activity, and for one who was somewhat corpulent and already past the prime of life, he had considerable stamina. Sometimes, however, he found he could not keep up the pace of a youngster, and he would be forced to slip away for a rest. But he was soon back, reinvigorated, and with a chuckle he would dig me in the ribs to intimate that he was ready for more. Christmas would not have been Christmas without him.

In addition to his other avuncular virtues, Uncle Jim had a fund of good stories, too, with a different war to reminisce over, for he had served with a Yeomanry Regiment in the South African War. It never occurred to me as a child that this was in any way a discreditable campaign. After all, were we children not taught at school that a long succession of military operations were made necessary by our national role as custodians of the greatest empire the world had ever known? Even if the thought had crossed my mind, it would have been dispelled quickly by the recollection that this, after all, had been the war for which my Uncle Jim had seen fit to offer his services.

Uncle Jim was a commercial traveller, and in his time he had travelled in just about every item of merchandise sold over the chemist's counter. Everyone who knew him said he was a very good commercial traveller, and I needed no convincing that they were right because, occasionally and as a special treat, he allowed me to accompany him on his selling sorties. I remember during one long, hot summer holiday, staying with my aunt and uncle at their flat in Ealing, and going around London with Uncle Jim in a diminutive 'Top Hat' Austin Seven, provided by a progressive and appreciative employer at a time when most commercial travellers had to use public transport. Everywhere we went he knew the exact location of each chemist's shop. At each one he approached the manager in a quiet, confiding manner — speaking to him more as a friend than as a mere representative of the commercial world — and putting forward cogent reasons why the products he was carrying were better than the manager had seen before, or would ever be likely to see again. Uncle Jim's smooth-tongued advocacy could be applied equally successfully to cosmetics, corn-plasters, sedatives or razor-blades, and orders filled his book as fast as he could write them.

It wasn't only when we met that Uncle Jim radiated good cheer in my direction. My boyhood was punctuated by a long succession of picture post-cards, sent by him from towns all over the country. Sometimes they would be Donald McGill comic-cards, sometimes views of the places he visited. From Great Yarmouth came a picture of 'Scotch fisher-lassies' addressed to: "Dear Spike, Very wet and fishy here", and from Portsmouth, a post-card of 'H.M.S. Victory' which was, he asserted on the back: "The best view in Portsmouth". The brightest of all the cards were those that offered the prospect of an early meeting. From Exeter, with some views of the town, including one of an open-topped tramcar in Fore Street, he wrote: "All being well I hope to see your funny face on Sunday next", and from Liverpool, with a view of the Mersey Ferry: "Dear Spike, Hope to see you tomorrow, so get the 'dope' ready, perhaps we may go to the 'talkies' if a good one on".

* * * * *

The 'talkies' were all the rage then, the sound of the human voice having added a new dimension to 'going to the pictures'. For three decades the cinema had been dominated by its mute idols, whose captioned words — aided by musical accompaniment from the cinema orchestra — took the place of speech. Birmingham had acquired its first cinema in 1901 at the Curzon Hall — later the West End Cinema — where the 'New Century Animated Pictures' were screened. Within a few years picture houses were mushrooming all around the town and suburbs, and in 1916 the Exchequer, taking note of what had already become a burgeoning national industry, first imposed an entertainment tax upon it.

I remember the thrill of cinema-going in the still silent days of the 'twenties, and some of the rare characters who had become legends almost overnight. Most memorable were Douglas Fairbanks and Mary Pickford, the quintessentially romantic figures of the silent screen; Harold Lloyd, whose daring acrobatics earned him the title of the 'human fly'; the poker-faced and enigmatic Buster Keaton; Jackie Coogan, the endearing waif; and that unforgettable dog, Rin-Tin-Tin, known in the film industry as the 'mortgage-lifter' because of his fantastic box-office draw. Best of all I remember Charlie Chaplin in 'The Gold Rush', when Chaplin, the starving gold prospector, cooks his old boot before eating the lace as if it were spaghetti, and the sole like a luscious steak.

The Globe Cinema, High Street, Aston, known originally as the Globe Electric
Theatre, stood almost opposite the Barton's Arms.   *from a sketch by C.V. Cox*
See Chapter 4.

The end of the silent era came quite suddenly and as something of a shock to cinema-goers when, in 1929, the silence was broken by Al Jolson, crooning 'Sonny Boy' in the all-talking, all-singing film, 'The Singing Fool', described by one commentator of the time as a penetrating and vulgar mammy-song. But the mass-appeal of sound was obvious from the length of the queues outside those cinemas supplying it. The 'talkies' had come to stay.

*　*　*　*　*

My parents were not very politically minded. I suppose they were always 'Tories' for the simple reason that their bread and butter depended on private enterprise. I remember how Mrs. Potterton — a kindly woman who came to my home once a week to help my mother with the housework, and who sometimes stayed with me when my parents went out at night — was said to be, like her husband, a Labour supporter. This somehow stigmatised them, but I hadn't the faintest idea why, any more than I could work out at a later stage how boys at school said to be 'Catholics' or 'Jews' were in some way different from the rest. Against this background it is, perhaps, not surprising that the General Strike of 1926 should have held no great significance for me.

Just before it started, however, my father — who always had what might be called 'literary aspirations' — wrote some verses of a topical nature, entitled 'The Miner', which appeared in the 'Daily Express':

> Shovel and Pick, and Safety Lamp.
> > Seven hours or more, and a feeling of cramp.
> Dynamite, Pit-props, Tubs and Rails.
> > All the way from Lanark to Wales.
>
> Subsidies, Deadlocks, Commissions,
> > Reports on our work and conditions.
> 'Hotheads' and others who try to beguile us,
> > Solemn-faced critics who sometimes revile us.
>
> Fire-damp, 'falls' and runaway tubs,
> > Hazards of gas, and hospitable pubs,
> Seek to engulf us. Do we complain?
> > Well, no. You see, we're out of the rain.

I was impressed by my father's poetic burgeoning, but at eight years of age I lacked any comprehension of its implications, particularly the 'Subsidies, Deadlocks, Commissions' line.

It was, I found out later, a government threat to end a subsidy to the coal industry which had led to the private mine-owners making it known that they intended to reduce the wages and increase the working hours of the miners. A commission had been set up, which condemned subsidies, and which elected to retain the same working hours at a lower rate of pay. Under threat of closure of any pits which did not pay their way, the pit-owners accepted the commission's recommendations. The miners rejected the package, and deadlock followed.

Under the slogan 'Not a minute on the day, not a penny off the pay', the miners won massive trade union support for their cause, which culminated in the General Strike. During the nine days of the strike, urban dwellers had the novel experience of having their trams and 'buses operated by volunteers — mainly professional men and undergraduates — and of seeing all manner of people performing unfamiliar jobs in the cause of keeping things moving. Schoolmasters became special constables, a lord was reported to have been driving a train, and under the Emergency Powers a large convoy of lorries, escorted by a battalion of Grenadier Guards with armoured cars was sent from Hyde Park to the London Docks to pick up stocks of flour lying there, the removal of which had previously been obstructed by strikers.

The General Strike was called off by the T.U.C. after nine days, but transport workers, dockers and printers remained out for a further five days, and the miners for another six months before returning to work — for less money and longer hours.

My only clear recollection of the event was of waiting with my mother at the 'King's Head', Hagley Road for a lift into Birmingham, because the trams were not running. Some of the prosperous occupants of the large Victorian and Georgian houses along Hagley Road would, no doubt, have been glad if the trams had stayed off for good, for they were always thought to have lowered the tone of that august thoroughfare, and opposition to them was long-standing. Broad Street's campaign against the tramcar had been more successful than that of Hagley Road, for largely through the efforts of Robert Lee and George Longland, partners in the firm of Lee, Longland Ltd., of Broad Street, the route of the trams to Five Ways from the city was deflected from Broad Street by way of John Bright Street, Holloway Head, Bath Row and Islington Row, and on their return journey to their Navigation Street terminus they traversed Suffolk Street instead of John Bright Street, so avoiding the need for double track in either of those thoroughfares.

This was called 'loop running' and was a device much used by Birmingham's tramway planners. There were loops taking trams round the Council House extension at Margaret Street, Edmund Street and Congreve Street; at Snow Hill there was another, taking the trams around Snow Hill Station; and a further one 'looping' Corporation Street by way of Martineau Street and James Watt Street. Albert Street, High Street and Carrs Lane formed yet another loop, while in Balsall Heath there was a labyrinth of single track running, resulting in the 'up' and the 'down' tracks being in different streets for the greater part of the journey through that district and in local people calling it the 'Chinese railway'.

In those hard-up days of the 'twenties and 'thirties, a tram ticket was often a passport to somewhere interesting but not too far from home. For 5d., 2d. for children, (2p. and 1p. respectively), one could take the tram from Navigation Street and go the whole length of the Bristol Road, rocking and rolling along miles of track-reservation, to the Lickeys. A shorter, and cheaper, tram-ride from the city was to Cannon Hill Park, and from my home, boarding a tram at the 'King's Head', it was just a few minutes ride to the 'Ivy Bush', from whence it was another five minutes on foot to the Botanical Gardens in Westbourne Road. Those enchanted acres of landscaped rusticity were, and still are, a living memorial to John Claudius Loudon, who, planned, laid out and planted the gardens in 1831, when he spent six weeks in the town with his wife.

Loudon, a Scotsman, was a landscape gardener, botanist and architect, whose work was highly regarded in Victorian times. He was described as that rare breed 'a Scot without business instincts' and, typically, he asked for no fee for the labour of love which he performed at Edgbaston and was, as a result, only paid the expenses to cover his visit.

*   *   *   *   *

The Botanical Gardens Edgbaston, from a Victorian print.

My first school was in Gillott Road, a name commemorating local connections with that nineteenth century Prince of Penmakers, Joseph Gillott. Each morning my mother would walk with me from Bearwood, down the Hagley Road or, on wet days, we would take the No. 34 tram from the 'King's Head'. At the corner of Hagley Road and Gillott Road she would leave me to complete the last few hundred yards of the journey alone. This I did with a heavy heart, for I had led a singularly sheltered life, and school, or the thought of it, filled me with nervous forebodings.

Fortunately for me, however, my fears were usually allayed on arrival. Miss Smith, who ran the establishment unaided, was

23

kindness itself, and did her good-natured best to dispense the rudiments of learning to a more than somewhat snobbish clientele of pampered young Edgbastonians, (except for me, of course, who, coming from Bearwood, had nothing to be snobbish about). The snobbishness was exemplified by Anthony, who didn't approve of the current hit-song of the day: 'It Ain't Gonna Rain no Mo'!' because, he pronounced in a haughty voice: "It should be 'It *Isn't* Going to Rain *any* More!' "

The learning at Miss Smith's school was sketchy, and the only subject which made any impression on me was history, which Miss Smith enlivened with stories and anecdotes, designed to clothe the bare bones of the long dead with flesh and blood and — what was more important — to give them emotions and feelings which were immediately understandable to a young child. Good manners were assiduously cultivated, and when my mother came to meet me after school, Miss Smith, if within earshot, would always remind me to doff my cap to her, and the habit became so engrained that I extended the same courtesy to all and sundry, including the postman and the dustman.

My next school was Wellesbourne, a private establishment, run by a formidable and autocratic woman, Miss Diaper. With some assistance from her sister, 'Miss Cissie', she organised the school along semi-military lines, and, to the strains of 'Onward Christian Soldiers', strummed out on an old piano, she was for ever marching her pupils through the upper rooms of the spacious house in which she practised her educational theories.

Those theories were classical rather than modern, for Miss Diaper had a penchant for the Greek concept of linking music with gymnastic exercises, to which she added her own brand of learning by rote. We chanted at her behest such near platitudes as 'An island is a piece of land entirely surrounded by water' and 'A cape is a head of land running into the sea' to the accompaniment of various gesticulations of the arms. This branch of learning appeared on term reports as 'Callisthenics', which was even less useful than Miss Diaper's brand of French, consisting of mouthing a few faltering phrases in that language to her supercilious Pekinese. The comments on the reports were written by Miss Diaper in an ostentatious hand in purple ink.

The best thing about Wellesbourne was its location. Standing on high ground in Beech Lanes — better known as Hagley Road West — it faced the extension of Lightwoods Park and commanded a view across

Beech Lanes 1927, near King's Head showing corner removed shortly afterwards for road improvements.   Photo: Sidney Smith

still open country to the rear. Beside Wellesbourne there was a stile, marking the commencement of a path across the fields to Harborne, and behind the house was a large rambling garden where, in summer, the school sports were held. A few yards along the road from Wellesbourne in the direction of Birmingham were the huge beech trees which gave aptness to the names of Beech Lanes and nearby Beechwood Road.

I remember coming out of school one afternoon in the fall of 1926, and with what elation I kicked my way through a carpet of fallen leaves as I crossed a traffic-free Beech Lanes, beneath the still dark canopy of the trees. I had left Wellesbourne for the last time. A few days later we moved from Bearwood into a new house in Wylde Green, Sutton Coldfield.

The Parade Sutton Coldfield in 1928

Both 'wylde' and 'green' were, at that time, apt epithets for a place of lingering rusticity, still a good many years away from being enveloped by spreading suburbia. Hedgerows and trees bounded fields where the horse still drew the plough; where, in spring, lark and cuckoo constantly made their presence heard; and where the onset of autumn was marked by the appearance of flocks of lapwings, mingling with the foraging rooks.

Our move to Wylde Green coincided with my father changing his job, when he found it necessary to have a telephone installed to enable him to deal with business matters from the comfort of his own hearth. The 'phone was an elegant device on a box-type stand, with a handle on the side for turning to call the operator, through whom all calls had to be made, automation being still a refinement of the future. There were less than a thousand subscribers in Sutton Coldfield in 1926, (our number was 'Sutton 964'), and perhaps because of this, and the fact that one didn't know anyone to ring, the telephone played no part in our private lives.

In addition to a new house and a telephone, we had electric lighting instead of gas. Sutton Coldfield Corporation Electricity Department generated its own power in those days, and electricity in the home was matched by electric street lamps. For several years, however, we had no lamps at all in our still semi-rural surroundings. When they were eventually installed they were lit each night by a lamplighter who came round on a push-bike, carrying a long pole with a little hook at the end for switching them on individually.

My father's new status was also reflected in his acquisition of a large, flat-topped desk, the top of which, as well as the drawers, soon became a mass of seemingly unco-ordinated papers. The middle drawer of the desk was usually kept locked, and I often wondered what it contained. One day, finding it unlocked, my curiosity got the better of me, and I had a look inside. I saw there a plain-covered copy of 'The Decameron Tales' by Boccaccio, which puzzled me at first, but when I scanned through its pages, it occurred to me that my father must have hidden it away because be considered it to be unsuitable reading for a ten-year-old.

Superimposed upon the wildness and greenness of Wylde Green was a red rash of house-building, and — like the other small boys who had moved into the locality — I soon became involved in various activities only made possible by the presence of building sites and material. I climbed ladders; I jumped from joist to joist in floorless upper rooms; I attempted to cross lime-pits by spanning them with scaffold-poles and walking across, arms akimbo — sometimes with messy results. I liked nothing better than to join the 'brickies' and the 'chippies' in their shanty when they were brewing tea. "Ei up, 'ere's the gaffer!" was the sign for beating a hasty retreat, for 'the gaffer', Mr. James — the builder of our new house — was a fearsome old gentleman with a bristling white moustache, whose anger was measured to strike fear into the hearts of intruders, especially small boys.

Mr. James may have been fearsome, but he had, it seemed, another side to his nature. During the 1914-1918 War, so the story went, he had, as a part-time farmer, made a contract with the army authorities to collect pig-swill from the military camps then in Sutton Park. At one stage he found that a lot of the swill consisted of jam rolls, roly-poly puddings and cakes. He arranged for these items to be segregated hygienically, following which he was to be seen outside his home in Whitehouse Common Road, Sutton Coldfield, distributing the fare to poor children on their way to school. Unfortunately, however, the children were arriving at school in so sticky a state that the headmistress had to ask Mr. James if he could defer his distribution of largesse until the children were on their way home at night.

My own education was resumed shortly after our move to Wylde Green, when I was sent to the elementary school down the lane, where I came under the care and guidance of Mr. William Prothero, the headmaster. He directed my unwilling steps to the classroom of Standard 2, then in charge of his fellow-Welshman, 'Bunk' Jones, a kindly, bearded, brisk-moving little man of advancing years, whose minor eccentricities delighted his pupils. Every morning 'Bunk' would be accompanied to school by a trail of small boys as he invariably rushed at breakneck speed along Sheffield Road and over the footbridge across the railway and into Green Lanes. In his headlong flight he would undo his waistcoat for no obvious reason, then, like the White Rabbit in 'Alice in Wonderland', do it up again, take his watch from his pocket, peer at it, and rush on at an even faster pace, leaving his young followers breathless before they had reached their destination.

Kindly was not the first word to spring to mind in speaking of Mr. Prothero, but he was, without doubt, a man to be respected. Tall and powerfully built, his ability to prevent small boys from becoming

Standard 6, Green Lanes Boy's School c.1930. The teacher was Mr. Clinton. The author is third from the right in the front row.

juvenile delinquents was based on a keen eye, sound psychology and an impressive dexterity with the cane. At the time of my first meeting with him, he was a man in the prime of life who, silently shod in crêpe soled shoes, moved around the school with as little sound as a Sioux Indian Chieftain. His prey was small boys in the act of deviating from the somewhat rigid behaviour-pattern to which small boys were then expected to conform. His approach to the classroom was frequently heralded by the appearance of his dark, sleekly-brushed head when, rising slowly to his full height, he would peer above the partition separating classroom from assembly-hall. This was often the first and only intimation the miscreant had of his lurking presence before retribution overtook him.

'The Gaffer', as all the boys called Mr. Prothero, was not above the use of guile when the necessity arose, as on the occasion of a frenzied spell of scribbling on hallowed walls in copying-ink pencil and a childish hand. Following the offence he came into the classroom, exuding a quite unexpected degree of Celtic charm, and after chatting to us on a variety of subjects, he indicated that, for a project he had in mind, he wanted to borrow a copying-ink pencil. The ruse worked. The culprit offered to lend him the instrument of his guilt, and duly paid the penalty for his credulity. Corporal punishment with Mr. Prothero didn't only include the cane. Another incident involving the use of a copying-ink pencil occurred when a boy named Jimmie badly marked the back of my jacket. My mother complained to Mr. Prothero about it, and he, having called Jimmie from his class and obtained a confession from him, boxed his ears in my mother's presence. This incident caused her considerable distress, and for years afterwards, whenever she saw Jimmie, she would go out of her way to intercept him for the purpose of giving him a copper or two.

Mr. Prothero had two ruling passions. The one was the desire to instil in our embryonic intellects a quite unnatural interest in and ability to solve all manner of arithmetical problems. The 'three Rs' as far as he was concerned were listed in the wrong order. 'Reading, Writing and Arithmetic' was an affront to his sense of priorities. His other passion was for sport, and any measure of success on the part of the school's football team was the occasion for much rejoicing and back-slapping. When it wasn't football, it was cricket, and the boys who were maladroit at ball games, (I was one of them), were expected to make some sort of showing on Sports Day or at the swimming baths. He had no time for those who were frightened of the water. Once, on finding a boy hiding in one of the cubicles, he threw him into the baths for his timidity.

'Gaffer' Prothero was not usually to be caught napping, but on one occasion, shortly after having admonished us for not looking where we were going as we marched up Green Lanes, en route for Sutton, he — in looking back for mischief in the rear of the column — collided forcibly with a roadside tree. Marches from the school to King Edward Square in Sutton Coldfield were not infrequent. Armistice Day on 11th November, with its universally observed 'two minutes silence' in memory of the dead of the Great War, was an annual commemoration which had some relevance to children, the majority of whom were 'war babies', born between 1914 and 1918. Most of us were imbued with an awareness of the awfulness of war, and it was constantly being drummed into us that 'it must not happen again' — an attitude which was responsible for a certain ambivalence in the minds of the young men of a decade later at the renewed outbreak of war.

Another 'civic occasion' in the 'twenties was Empire Day on 24th May. This was time for 'taking stock' and listening to speeches by civic dignitaries, as well as our teachers, on the nation's exalted role at the head of the greatest empire the world had ever seen — the empire upon which, we were told, the sun never set.

One event took place while I was at Green Lanes School which somehow seemed to symbolise this feeling of national greatness, instilled into us by our mentors. It was the only time as far as I can remember, too, when Mr. Prothero lost his sense of decorum. One morning he dashed into our classroom, eyes ablaze with excitement, and shouted to us, commanding us to rush outside if we wanted to see a sight we had never seen before. We needed no second bidding, and made for the playground as though the school were on fire. It was, indeed, a sight we had never seen before and, as it so happened, one we were not to see again. High in the sky, glistening and gleaming in the morning sun, was the huge silver hull of the R.101 airship, on a test flight from her mooring at Cardington in Bedfordshire.

A short while afterwards the great dirigible, described in the press as being as large as the 'Mauretania', set out on what was to have been her maiden flight to India. She left Cardington at dusk on Saturday, 4th October, 1930, and at about midnight was spotted by an elderly Frenchman, Eugene Rabouille, who was poaching rabbits on the edge of a wood near Beauvais in Northern France. The weather was wet and wretched, and as the huge airship, its passengers' quarters brightly lit, loomed into the Frenchman's view, there was a sudden violent squall, which caused it to dip its nose several times before crashing beside the wood. Simultaneously, there was a tremendous explosion, which knocked Rabouille to the ground, following which flames, hundreds of feet high, leaped into the night sky.

Dazed and shocked beyond endurance, the Frenchman ran home to bed. It was only later, when he realised that he was probably the sole witness to one of the great disasters of the age, that he came forward to testify to what he had seen. The only survivors were some passengers in part of a gondola which struck a tree and was ripped off. Everyone else, including the Air Minister and a number of airship experts from his ministry, were burned to death when the hydrogen ignited.

*　*　*　*　*

The Gate Inn, Boldmere Road, Sutton Coldfield, June 1938. Now the site of the Boldmere Hotel.　　　　*Photo: E.M. Sargeant*

I am an Anglican solely by token of having been baptised as an infant at the local parish church. The only time I remember going to church as a young child was when I was taken to the wedding of a neighbour's relative, but soon after moving to Wylde Green, my father decided he wanted to attend a nearby Baptist Chapel, and my mother and I went, too. I found no pleasure in being cloistered within those dark walls for an hour and a half at the end of my Sabbath daytime activities out in the sun and fresh air. Fortunately this chapel-going phase was only of short duration, for it seemed to serve finally to rid my father of any lingering orthodoxy, and thereafter he gave his allegiance to free-thought and many of the views propounded by the Rationalist Press.

My father's acceptance of the scientific and evolutionary explanation of the mysteries of creation played no small part in colouring my own vision of life. My sympathies towards his views increased when he acquired a microscope, a second-hand but beautiful instrument in a polished wooden cabinet. My interest was quickened in an infinity of life so small that I had hitherto not known of its existence and I became aware of the aptness of the couplet:

> Great fleas have little fleas upon their
> backs to bite 'em,
> And little fleas have lesser fleas,
> and so ad infinitum.

At the other end of the scale I discovered astronomy for myself, and was staggered by the revelation that many of those twinkling denizens of the night sky were so remote that their images, projected through the vast emptiness of space, took thousands of years to reach our tiny planet. I read everything I could get hold of on the subject and became aware, if vaguely, of the discoveries of Copernicus, Galileo, Kepler and Tycho Brahe. But I had no access to a telescope, nor did I find a mentor to point out to me the planets and constellations, and their whereabouts in the heavens remained a mystery to me.

*   *   *   *   *

When we moved to our new home, my father had to contend with an old field-hedgerow, which ran diagonally across the garden. In grubbing it up and clearing the site, he looked to me for assistance, with the result that certain limitations were placed on my free time. I was often told that I could only go out to play with other boys after I had done a stint in the garden. Surprisingly, this discipline did not turn me against gardening. On the contrary, my interest in it grew as, over the years, the layout and planting developed under my father's inspired efforts.

My pleasure in seeing the garden take shape may have been associated in my mind with my very early recollections of the Shakespeare Gardens in Lightwoods Park near my old home. That beautiful walled and secluded haven, containing as it did then some

33

200 plants and flowers mentioned in Shakespeare's works, had given me horticultural standards.

> *. . . Here's flowers for you;*
> *Hot lavender, mints, savory, marjoram,*
> *The marigold, that goes to bed wi' the sun,*
> *And with him rises weeping . . . .*

and above all, the roses, silk-soft and sensually fragrant. The ultimate goal of gardening, I felt, was no mystery to me.

Beyond our garden there were fields extending to the railway embankment of the Sutton and Four Oaks branch line, strewn in summer with wild flowers, and beyond the railway, more fields as far as Boldmere Road. There was a pathway, spanned by a bridge, under the railway, used by the farmer and his men to take their carts and farm implements to and from fields on either side of the track. The level of the land had been lowered at this point and local boys always called the hollow 'Devil's Ditch', which became a rendez-vous and hide-out as well as a focal-point for a variety of activities. Train-spotting; cow-boys and Indians; tip-cat; five-stones; conkers and other diversions filled the wide-margined days of childhood.

Involvement in the activities of the farmer's year was an extra bonus. Ploughing and reaping were undertaken with the horse as prime-mover, and it was not unusual to see one farm-labourer plant a whole field of potatoes by hand. Harvest-time, whether of root-crop or grain, offered us local boys the chance to make a few coppers. Collecting potatoes was one of the jobs where casual labour was welcome, but the harvesting of wheat or barley was much more fun. There were no combine harvesters, and the golden grain was cut by reaping machine, which bound it into sheaves. When the sheaves were spewed out of the machine, they were gathered up by whatever labour could be mustered, and stacked in 'stooks', seven or eight sheaves to the stook. The reaping machine, working its way from the field's perimeter towards the middle, would eventually reduce the area to be cut to a tiny rectangle of standing grain in the middle of the field. When this was finally cut there was a hasty exodus and a frenzied scattering in all directions of rabbits, hares, mice and voles, dispossessed and disorientated by the harvest. I always felt sympathy for the poor

The Sutton and Four Oaks branch line in 1932 showing 'Devil's Ditch', a rendez-vous and hideout for small boys.
Photo: Douglas V. Jones

creatures and, thinking perhaps of Bobbie Burns' mouse, turned up in her nest by the plough:

> *Wee, sleekit, cow'rin', tim'rous beastie . . .*

I never had any inclination to club or bludgeon them, as was sometimes the practice.

*   *   *   *   *

Early in 1928 the local press drew attention to the fact that Sutton Coldfield was about to celebrate the 400th anniversary of the granting of its Royal Charter by King Henry VIII. This charter was granted by

The "Royal Town" sign just beyond the Erdington tram terminus, 1938
Photo: E.H. Sargeant

the king as a token of his goodwill towards his friend and confidant, John Harman, alias Bishop Vesey, a native of the town. The mayor of Sutton Coldfield made it known that he thought all the town's inhabitants should take part in commemorating the occasion, and despite a sharp division in the council chamber, £1,000 was allocated for the celebrations in the form of a pageant.

John Willmott, a member of the council, declared that the pageant would lead to what he called 'the quickening of local patriotism and the deepening of interest in the town's history' and he volunteered to produce and write the episodes. The much publicised event took place in Sutton Park in July, 1928, and the opening was attended by an estimated 6,000 spectators and a number of V.I.Ps. Almost 1,200 performers took part in the pageant, which told Sutton Coldfield's story through the centuries from Roman times.

Whatever else the Sutton Pageant of 1928 did or did not achieve, it certainly fulfilled John Willmott's prediction by 'quickening local patriotism and increasing interest in the town's history'. Many of us who were young then probably first became aware of history at a purely local level as a result of it.

History at school in those days often consisted of learning by rote the dates of English kings from Norman times onwards, and listening to a few well-aired anecdotes such as how William Rufus met his death in the New Forest, and the circumstances under which King John lost the Crown Jewels in the Wash. In 1928 we found out for the first time that Sutton Coldfield, a community with a population of 27,000 inhabitants, possessed a long and colourful history, distinct from that of any other town in England. To prove it, it had a Roman road skirting the western fringe of its 2,400 acre park, preserved for posterity through the good offices of an erring and devious prelate — Vesey, Bishop of Exeter, the town's benefactor.

*   *   *   *   *

We didn't see many foreigners in Birmingham during the 'twenties and 'thirties. Occasionally a Frenchman, wearing a beret, would come to the door, carrying a string of onions; very infrequently one would see a black man in the street, but even in London foreigners were not very numerous. As a consequence, xenophobia hardly existed, the strongest emotion of the Englishman towards visitors from overseas being that of mild curiosity. The British Empire spanned the earth, and its beneficent role was, we were encouraged to believe, self-evident. Children, of course, only knew it vicariously, chiefly by means of what they were taught at school. I had had the added advantage of having been taken by my mother to the British Empire Exhibition at Wembley in 1924, which, apart from being a spectacular pageant of Imperialism, had, in addition, the steepest 'Big Dipper' ever seen in England.

Empire building, we were taught at school, was not all plain sailing. Sometimes the natives did not know their own good fortune in being colonised by such enlightened people as the English. The Indians, for instance, had mutinied in 1857, but they had been quickly shown the folly of their ways, as had been the Zulus and the Fuzzy-Wuzzies later.

But Rudyard Ripling, that arch-poet of Imperialism, in his 'Barrack Room Ballads', reminded us that we didn't always win every round:

> ... 'ere's to you Fuzzy-Wuzzy, at your 'ome
> in the Soudan;
> You're a pore benighted 'eathen but a first-class
> fightin' man.
> An' 'ere's to you, Fuzzy-Wuzzy, with your 'ayrick
> 'ead of 'air;
> You big black boundin' beggar — for you broke
> a British square!

The concept of Empire was enshrined in the Indian sub-continent, and at school we spend a lot of time studying the background to our domination over its population of 400,000,000. We learnt all about the East India Company, Clive's victory at Plassey, and the Indian Mutiny, but we knew no Indians, and our mental image of them alternated between the turbaned Indian menial on the Camp Coffee bottle in the act of serving coffee to a kilted Highland officer, sitting outside his tent, and a sparse, bespectacled little brown-skinned man, who came to London as his country's representative, wearing only a loin-cloth and a bland smile — Mohandas Gandhi.

* * * * *

CHAPTER II

Books and Birds

*I never let schooling interfere
with my education.*

Mark Twain

WHEN I WAS very young the comic strips of Tiger Tim, the Bruin Boys and Mr. Marzipan in 'Rainbow', together with those funny little monochrome characters in 'Chips' — Weary Willie and Tired Tim — limited the need for reading. But books were very much a part of my childhood home, and some of them aroused my curiosity. Graham Greene tells us: "I remember distinctly the suddenness with which a key turned in a lock and I found I could read — not just the sentences in a reading book with the syllables coupled like railway carriages, but a real book." I knew the feeling. Reading came to me as a joy and a revelation, as well as a source of entertainment.

The first book I ever read from cover to cover was Émile Zola's 'The Attack on the Mill'. It was one of my father's books, and my interest in it had been quickened by the frontispiece, showing an officer with a sword leading the attack, the gory details of which I felt I must know. Reading it was a landmark in my young life. James Barrie's 'Peter Pan' was a spell-binder in which the horrible Captain James Hook, with his double-pronged iron hook instead of a right hand, was only exceeded in horror by the crocodile which ate him. Grandma Jones sent me a copy of 'Alice in Wonderland', which I enjoyed as an alternative to 'What Katy Did' and the 'William' books of Richmal Crompton, while Rider Haggard, G.A. Henty, Fenimore Cooper and the Sherlock Holmes stories of Conan Doyle all contributed to my widening taste.

From time to time I sampled the 'Boys' Own Paper' and Arthur Mee's 'Children's Newspaper', but neither of them had, for me, the appeal of 'Modern Boy', which made its brief, meteoric appearance in the late

Penns Lane, Sutton Coldfield coming from Walmley and showing the Josiah Mason Orphanage at Erdington (demolished in 1964)
From a watercolour by C.V. Cox

'twenties. By far the most absorbing of the weeklies were 'The Magnet' and 'The Gem', which contained the school stories of that most prolific of writers, Charles Hamilton. His identity was hidden from his readers by the pen-names Martin Clifford, Owen Conquest and — perhaps best known of all — Frank Richards, under which name he created Greyfriars School, Billy Bunter, and all those upper-crust boys whose images and adventures were to create vicariously a public-school ethos for generations of boys of all classes.

When, in due course, I said farewell to Mr. Prothero and went to school in Aston my taste in books developed along positive lines.

Whether or not I owe this to my English-master, Mr. Lawrence, I cannot say. He was a heavy-jowled, corpulent man of advancing years, before whom I stood in some awe on account of his severity and sharp temper. But it was he who introduced me to facets of English literature, matching perfectly my growing interest in the open-air life, which was at that time prompting me to spend more and more of my free time roaming in Sutton Park and around the fields and hedgerows of Wylde Green and Walmley.

Through the pages of Palgrave's 'Golden Treasury' and under the guidance of Mr. Lawrence I first encountered the poetry of Wordsworth, Keats and Shelley and the matchless imagery of Thomas Gray's 'Elegy Written in a Country Churchyard'. One of the books chosen for 'special study' was R.L. Stevenson's 'Travels with a Donkey in the Cevennes', which showed me that prose-writing, too, was potentially no less evocative of the moods of nature than was poetry. The fastidious Mr. Lawrence did not approve of Stevenson as a man because, he said, he was lax in his personal habits, and his jacket was always marked with egg-stains. "A dirty man!" he would say, shaking his jowls disapprovingly as he made his pronouncement. But for me Stevenson was in a class apart. He was the first writer to show me how, by appealing to the inner eye of the reader, it was possible to transmit in words the mood of a river, rushing down a wild, pine-clad mountainside, or the loveliness of a night spent bivouacking under the stars, (escaping from the bastille of civilisation, as he called it):

> "Night is a dead monotonous period under a roof; but in the open world it passes lightly, with its stars and dews and perfumes, and the hours are marked by changes in the face of Nature. What seems a kind of temporal death to people choked between walls and curtains, is only a light and living slumber to the man who sleeps afield. . ."

Stevenson's words remained with me and I had many future opportunities, under both familiar and alien skies, of proving the truth of his assertion. I was encouraged henceforward to find other writers for myself with comparable qualities to Stevenson, and 'English literature' assumed a new meaning for me from that time onwards.

At Aston I acquired some small knowledge of the French language, learning as I did so to read the warranty, then appearing in French as well as in English, on the H.P. Sauce bottles:

Cette sauce de premier choix possède les plus hautes qualités digestives . . . .

H.P. Sauce was always associated in my mind with school-days at Aston, for its pungent smell, emanating from the Midland Vinegar Company's factory at Aston Cross, filled the air over a wide area with its heady aroma, dependent only in degree on which way the wind was blowing. The reason for the linguistic innovation of printing the warranty in French was obscure, but since it was first done during the Great War, when vast amounts of the sauce were sent to France to help in improving the flavour of bully-beef for the British troops, it may have been somebody's idea that the French nation might, with a little encouragement, be induced to buy the stuff.

There was more to Aston, of course, than H.P. Sauce and its many other commercial enterprises. It was a place with a distinguished past, reflected in the tall spire of its almost cathedral-like parish-church and the nearby Jacobean mansion, splendidly situated on a hill, the building of which was a 17-year project for Sir Thomas Holte in the early 17th century. When, as a boy, I first entered Aston Hall, history came vividly alive on seeing the great shattered staircase, hit by a Roundhead cannonball in 1643.

Despite the fact that Birmingham was an anti-Royalist stronghold -- described by a writer of the time as 'the abominably wicked town of Bromwicham' — Holte was an ardent supporter of the king, and the damage to the hall was caused when it was garrisoned with Royalist troops. It was besieged by the Parliamentarians, and after two days of combat, Sir Thomas was forced to surrender, when he was taken prisoner. He survived his ordeal and lived to the ripe old age of 83, outliving all his 15 children with the exception of one.

He was a proud, obstinate and quick-tempered man, and a widely circulated story told of how he murdered his cook. This was said to have happened at the Manor House of Duddeston, which was his family seat before the building of Aston Hall. The alleged crime was supposed to have taken place when, after having been out hunting, Sir Thomas boasted to his friends of his cook's punctuality. Unfortunately for the cook, however, he was late with the dinner on this occasion, and the enraged knight is said to have struck his poor servant with a cleaver, causing his head to be 'clove in twain'.

*　　*　　*　　*　　*

Maths was never my cup of tea, and at Aston my inability to comprehend the subject was matched by some degree of obscurity of expression on the part of Mr. Smith, the Maths Master. He was an elderly, unworldly man, and the only time that he spelt out a message for me was when he deviated from his subject, (which he frequently did), and with a faraway look in his eye, would expatiate at length on the joys and rewards of exploring the countryside by bike. The purest joy, according to Mr. Smith, was, having cycled along the highways and into the by-ways of England, to lift one's cycle over a stile and take the footpath way into a world, peaceful beyond all understanding. How I longed for a bike! But my parents insisted I must wait until I could pay for it myself.

So, by the irony of things, both English and Maths provided me with a mental escape-hatch into the world of nature, which attracted me more strongly each passing day. I steeped myself in country lore, and some of the knowledge which I could not acquire by practical means, I gained by voracious reading. My mentors became Gilbert White, Richard Jefferies and W.H. Hudson. Gilbert White, an 18th century cleric, was curate of Selborne in Hampshire and author of 'A Natural History of Selborne'. His quiet dedication, spanning 50 years, to the observation and meticulous recording of the wild life around his native village left an indelible impression upon me and, like the Muslim whose thoughts turn to going on pilgrimage to Mecca, I felt that Selborne was a place I must visit at least once in my lifetime.

Gilbert White's famous book — said to be the fourth most published work in the English language — was written in the form of letters addressed to friends with similar interests to his own. It contains his observations on everything he saw or heard around Selborne: fossil shells, toads, adders, squirrels, red deer, fruit, mushrooms, the comings and goings of the birds, and Timothy, his tortoise, of which he noted that: "There is a season of the year when his exertions are remarkable. He then walks on tiptoe and is stirring by five in the morning . . . The motives that impel him to undertake these rambles seem to be of the amorous kind; his fancy then becomes intent on sexual attachments, which transport him beyond his usual gravity and induce him to forget for a time his ordinary solemn deportment".

Richard Jefferies, writing a century after Gilbert White, gave his own inspired vision of the English countryside through the pages of his books, written in a style of sensuous beauty. He described himself as 'a student of nature and human life', which claim he justified again and again by his vivid portrayal of both the natural scene and the human condition.

By far my favourite author, however, was W.H. Hudson, whose limpid style prompted another writer to comment: "One cannot tell how this fellow gets his effects; he writes as the grass grows". Hudson was born of American parents in the Argentine, and was almost 30 before he set foot in England. But in the long life left to him he wrote more tellingly about the English rural scene than anyone else, before or since, and captured for posterity that lost world of around the turn of the century, before life had changed its tempo to adjust to the technological revolution.

* * * * *

Sutton Coldfield did not acquire its first public library until 1937, and many of the books which I read were borrowed from the Free Library in Erdington, which I joined when I was fourteen. Erdington library, which was built in 1907, was not paid for out of public funds. It was financed by Andrew Carnegie, the philanthropist, whose benefactions, both here and in America, exceeded £70 million. Erdington was one of many libraries in Britain and the United States paid for by Carnegie, who was born in Scotland and who emigrated to America in 1848. He worked there as a factory-hand, and knew the meaning of real poverty before eventually founding the largest iron and steel works in America.

Among my father's books I discovered the Selected Poems of John Drinkwater, and in a poem, 'The Vagabond', I read:

> I know the pools where the grayling rise,
> I know the trees where the filberts fall,
> I know the woods where the red fox lies,
> The twisted elms where the brown owls call.

Even though I lived within four walls I was able to find similar happiness in knowing where to flush a snipe or hear the first chiffchaff in spring and in which thicket the wood-anemones flowered, and my visits to Sutton Park were made in all seasons and in all kinds of weather.

Bringing home the Christmas holly from Sutton Park, December 1938. A free supply of holly from the Park was one of the advantages of living in Sutton Coldfield.
Photo: E.H. Sargeant

In spring I would stroll beside Longmoor Brook, sparkling its way below Rowton's Bank, past the old well, once renowned for its medicinal waters due to an infusion of iron. Beyond Longmoor Pool — then possessing a little island where the grebes nested — I would follow the briskly flowing brook along the wooded perimeter of the Park towards Powells Pool, within sound of the willow-wren's cheery little song, ringing out from amid the soft, fresh greenery of the birch trees and with the distant voice of the cuckoo, drifting across from Holly Hurst.

Summer would see me beneath the great oaks of the Gumslade, the haunt of woodpeckers and nuthatches, where I would stand, enthralled by the flight of a green-woodpecker, its plumage as beautiful as a parrot's in the June sunshine. Along that other Park stream — the Ebrook — with spluttering bursts of whitethroat song emerging from the thick marginals and with swallows overhead, pursuing their day-long quest for tiny insects on the wing, I shared the sentiment of W.H. Davies, the tramp-poet:

> *What is this life if, full of care,*
> *We have no time to stand and stare.*
> *No time to stand beneath the boughs*
> *and stare as long as sheep or cows . . .*

In autumn I would watch the warm colours of the declining year bring a new vision of beauty to the Park, when the silver filigree of the birch boles was matched by the gold of their leaves, and the bracken, of a deeper gold, stood almost six feet tall. Winter, too, beneath a leaden sky and with the Park blanketed in snow, brought its own enjoyment: that of silence, broken only by the isolated sounds emanating from a dormant landscape. Those sounds, I discovered, being few, were more easily identified than the many sounds of summer — the harsh croak of a passing carrion-crow, the distant bark of a dog, the remote rattle of a far-away train and the gentle twitter of a green linnet, flying overhead, all served to emphasise an otherwise silent world.

*   *   *   *   *

My reading was not all geared to the enhancement of my love of nature. I dipped into books of all kinds. The true bookworm will read anywhere, oblivious to either the presence or the absence of his fellow-men. I have read on trams, 'buses, trains, in bed, on picnics and — during the war — on troop-ships, in trucks crossing the desert and in hospital. Whether or not my taste for books was unusual in a youth of my age and background, I did not know, and I rarely indicated to my friends that I was one of those queer characters who made a habit of carrying a book in his jacket pocket. The early Penguin paperbacks, which only cost sixpence (2½p) in the 'thirties, were a boon to people like me.

Some of my parents' books appealed to me greatly, particularly a small leather-bound edition of Charles Lamb's 'Essays of Elia' and

"Lichfield, with its statues of Johnson, sitting on his plinth, looking ruefully towards his birthplace across the then cobbled market-place, and a few yards away, the cock-a-hoop sprightly Boswell, became for me a town of vivid literary associations".

James Boswell's 'The Life of Samuel Johnson'. Charles Lamb, for 33 years a clerk with the East India Company, custodian of his poor demented sister, who has stabbed their mother to death in a bout of madness, and himself a victim of depression was, despite his troubles, capable in some of his essays of a warmth and a shared intimacy with his reader probably unsurpassed in the English language.

It took me several weeks to read 'The Life of Samuel Johnson', but as far as I was concerned it was time well spent. Thanks to the rare genius of that comical little toady, Boswell, I became on nodding terms with the inimitable Doctor Johnson and all those friends and acquaintances of his, whose lively presence has been preserved within the book's covers for the delight of readers down the ages. It was, for me, a happy coincidence that Johnson's hometown was so near to Sutton Coldfield. Lichfield, with its statues of Johnson, sitting on his plinth, looking ruefully towards his birthplace across the then cobbled market-place, and a few yards away the cock-a-hoop sprightly Boswell, became for me a town of vivid literary associations.

My knowledge of the modern world was largely confined to what I had acquired from reading books by Stephen King-Hall and John Gunther, supplemented by political commentaries in the 'Sunday Times' — until, that is, I met Mildred. She was the first girl I had encountered with positive and forthright views on society and, like so many young people, she was being greatly influenced by the events of the Spanish Civil War, then being waged with great ferocity. Her reading differed considerably from my own. She was a member of the Left Book Book, and through her I became aware of the intellectual 'Left', as represented by such men as W.H. Auden, Stephen Spender, Cecil Day Lewis and Louis MacNeice, all of them poets and all of them deeply concerned with the problems of the age, following upon and largely arising from the Great War of two decades earlier.

One week a letter appeared in the correspondence column of the 'Sunday Times', in which someone enquired about the source of a quotation:

> "... I am no more lonely than the mill brook, or a weathercock, or the north star, or the south wind, or an April shower, or a January thaw, or the first spider in a new house."

From subsequent correspondence the source was revealed as being a book entitled 'Walden' or 'Life in the Woods' by Henry David Thoreau. The book, it was said, consisted of an account of building and living alone for two years in a shanty on the edge of Walden Pool in Concord, Massachusetts, an experiment Thoreau undertook in 1845, when he was able to put into practice his own theories relating to the simple life.

My interest was awakened, and I went foraging in the second-hand bookshops then to be found in John Bright Street and the Horse Fair. The penny-boxes were unproductive, but I managed to get a nice Victorian edition of 'Walden' for sixpence (2½p.), and I was soon under the spell of this New England guru. His whole philosophy, I found, was one of simplicity, in which he maintained that Man is constantly finding more and more things have become necessities, to acquire which he must work harder and harder so that, as a result, he has no time to savour the real pleasures of living in the 'here and now'. There was nothing impractical about Thoreau's life beside Walden Pool, for he earned his livelihood there entirely by the labour of his own hands, supplying his simple dietary needs by what he grew on a small plot of land beside his hut.

By accepted standards, Thoreau was a strange man. He lived 'on the fringe of society' but, as he reflected, if a man did not keep pace with his companions, perhaps it was because he heard a different drummer. Thoreau duly found his place beside Gilbert White, Richard Jefferies and W.H. Hudson on my bookshelf.

I felt that Selborne was a place I must visit at least once in my lifetime

Corporation Street, during Lewis's Summer Sale, 1930.

CHAPTER III

"Today we are going to look into the hearts of the flowers...."

Sex AND ITS various manifestations were rarely discussed, except with one or two of one's male companions. It was certainly not the explicit subject which it later became, and one never quite knew what the other fellow did when he 'dated' a girl, unless he told you, and even then you could not be sure that he was not spoofing. The 'facts of life' were facts which one only acquired little by little, and usually quite fortuitously over a long period of time and from a variety of sources. The process was something like doing a jig-saw puzzle in which, having got so far with it, one was held up by the difficulty of finding the appropriate pieces to fill in the gaps. But gradually the picture took shape, and the puzzle was solved.

When I was very young my mother had told me where babies came from, but not how they were conceived, or how they made their entry into the world. When I was somewhat older, Grandma Jones had sent me a slender volume called 'The Wonder of Life', subtitled 'A Talk with Children about Sex ', which began:

> "Today we are going to look into the hearts of the
> flowers and learn something about Life from them...."

but it was not until some time afterwards that I acquired any real knowledge of the procreative process at a purely human level. My mentor was my namesake, Douglas, a boy a year or so older than me, who lived in a house across the road. He seemed to know everything worth knowing on the subject, and had a certain flair for giving an edge to the information which he imparted. Once, I remember, in stressing the universal nature of the act of procreation, he took for an example

Mr. Hughes, an ageing and somewhat cadaverous-looking teacher and family man, known always among the boys as 'Crump'. "Why" exclaimed Douglas "even 'Crump' has done it!" When, later on, it came to courting, Douglas, on his own admission, was chivalrous, and turned to music for inspiration, by which means he claimed he had beguiled a number of girls into a romantic mood with his portable gramophone and an early recording of Bing Crosby, crooning 'Love in Bloom'.

Many of the boys I knew seemed very little better informed on life than I was. One person who contributed to our knowledge of the world, however, was Horace. He was a thick-set man in his mid-twenties, whose widowed mother kept a corner-shop about half a mile away from home. He had a barrel-chest, a 'lazy' eye and a laugh which could be best described as having a strong similarity to the laughing call of the green-woodpecker, ringing through a woodland glade on a summer's morning.

Because Horace was a bit of a character, we boys enjoyed cultivating his company, and he returned our friendship. When we were young he allowed us to ride on his greengrocery cart, which was pulled around the district by an ancient and rheumaticky horse, given to frequent bouts of wind. As we neared adolescence he took us into his confidence by telling us of his amatory adventures in the arms of a succession of servant-girls — of whom there were a good many in the district at the time — and after his mother's death these encounters, he said, usually took place in the living quarters behind the shop, which he had inherited.

Horace's laugh was infectious, and since he always enjoyed a joke, we did our best to accommodate him. One boy, Dennis, had the best stock of stories of anyone we knew, and he would sometimes go to the pictures with Horace. Sitting towards the back of the stalls he would, during the moments of highest drama, pour into Horace's receptive ear a succession of earthy anecdotes, causing the suspense to be punctuated from time to time by his penetrating cackle, to the consternation of other members of the audience.

*   *   *   *   *

CHAPTER IV

The Grand Cure

Work is the grand cure of all the maladies
and miseries that ever beset mankind.

Thomas Carlyle

I LEFT SCHOOL at midsummer, 1933, not yet sixteen and with no prospect of a job. It was a year of depression, recession and disillusionment. In England the unemployed reached a peak of almost three millions, for whom the bleakness of life was emphasised by the inquisitorial Means Test, introduced two years previously by the National Government headed by Ramsay MacDonald. In America things were no better, and the American Dream of 'a car in every garage and a chicken in every pot' was beginning to sound like a bad joke.

A World Economic Conference was convened for the purpose of stabilising currencies, but was wound up without having achieved its objective, and confidence in the League of Nations was ebbing. Hitler had come to power in Germany early in 1933, but he was not at the time taken too seriously, and his ascendency did little to dampen the ardour of the no-more-war brigade. Talks on pacifism and international disarmament reflected the popular mood, and defence cuts by the British Government were generally considered to be appropriate by a nation suffering from delayed shock following the horrific war of two decades earlier.

But life is for living, and the young are not too easily daunted by the state of the world and the conflicts and stresses within society. I didn't find society all that attractive, anyway, being, through shyness, fonder of my own company than that of others, and given to taking long, solitary walks.

Despite the fact that I had no taste for a sedentary job, and would

Birmingham was a city of trams in those days — almost 800 of them in fact.
Top: High Street, Erdington.   Bottom: Tram Terminus, Birchfield Road, Perr Barr.
Photos by W.A. Camwell

54

have preferred to have been working out of doors, I eventually got a post in a builder's and plumber's office in High Street, Aston, adjoining the Aston Hippodrome. I found myself working in a dark and stuffy office in which I spent much of each day calculating the cost of itemised estimates with a ready-reckoner. The plumbing estimates were particularly tedious, for many of the prices had farthings in them. The boredom defied description, and when I tried to relieve it by joining in the conversation which took place from time to time between two middle-aged men and Kitty, the typist, who occupied the same office, I was always told by the more forbidding of the two men to get on with my work. The hours were long, and the reward for a week's toil was just ten shillings, (50p.)

The bright spot of any week was when I was given a few coppers tram-fare and sent out on errands to various parts of the city. The feeling of having escaped was always very strong on such occasions, and I rarely hurried back. Birmingham was a city of trams in those days — over 800 of them in fact — but the twenty which ran along High Street, Aston, on the Perry Barr run were rather special ones. Built in 1904 and equipped with bogies, they were Birmingham Corporation's first electric tramcars, successors to the horse and steam trams. When later tramway extensions were made to the north of the city, these trams were too high to go under Aston Station Bridge. The new routes were, therefore, served by smaller, four-wheeled cars, leaving cars one to twenty, known as the 'Aston bogies', to ply permanently between the city and Perry Barr.

People born and bred in Aston still identified themselves with the mean streets in which they lived, and it was not necessary for do-gooders from outside to foster a community spirit among the hard-working indigenous population. It was already there. The focal-point of the community was the High Street, which was a lively enough thoroughfare in the early 'thirties, with plenty of small shops of every kind, a pawnbroker's, half-a-dozen or so pubs, a music-hall and two cinemas — one being a diminutive, *fin de siècle* building called the Globe Electric Theatre. Within spitting distance there were also two sizeable stores — The House that Jack Built in Newtown Row, and W.M. Taylor Ltd., on Potters Hill — which were often instrumental in saving Astonians from the need to go into Birmingham to shop. Just down the street from where I worked was a pork-butcher's shop, and adjoining it, a slaughter-house where, on the approach of a consignment of pigs to be slaughtered, they would squeal piteously in anticipation of their fate.

Kitty was a girl of 23, whose mother kept a tiny draper's shop on Potters Hill, where the family lived. She was fair, small featured and animated. She never tired of telling me what a smart office-boy my predecessor had been and how his enterprise, initiative and obvious ability had singled him out for a bright future. He had, Kitty pointed out, already taken a step in the right direction by leaving for a better paid job. Her intention may have been to goad a bashful and retiring youth into a more positive approach to life. Unfortunately her efforts had the reverse effect on my morale, but in deference to her views I did screw up enough courage to ask the manager for a rise. Much to my surprise he increased my wage by half-a-crown to twelve shillings and sixpence a week, but a short time later I had my sixteenth birthday, which meant I had to pay a contribution for my unemployment stamp. I complained to the manager of my financial setback, and I was fired.

*   *   *   *   *

Another, pleasanter reason for remembering that birthday was that it was the day on which I acquired my long-awaited bike. I had been saving what little I could from my meagre earnings, and when the day came my parents made up the difference, so enabling me to become the proud owner of a new Hercules cycle with 28 inch wheels and costing just under three pounds. My spell of unemployment was hardly long enough for me to feature in the astronomical statistics of the period, but sufficiently long to give me the opportunity to spend some pleasant hours cycling into the countryside around Birmingham. Christmas came and went, and my father, sick and tired of seeing me idle, said he would kick my backside if I didn't go in search of work immediately. I took the threat seriously, and duly presented myself at the Juvenile Employment Bureau in Margaret Street, Birmingham before the year ran out.

An official there decided that I was a suitable candidate for a vacancy as a junior clerk at the Head Office of what was then known as the Corporation Tramway and Omnibus Department in Birmingham's Council House. I was sent to see Mr. Ashby, a well-groomed, quietly spoken man of great dignity who was, I learned, the

Chief Accountant. To my surprise I found I was one of only three applicants for the post, due, I was told later, to lack of publicity. One of the other boys, being a Jew, was unable to work on Saturday mornings, the second, a bright, intelligent lad, had a stammer. My interview with Mr. Ashby went well. I told him I was no good at maths, he replied that it would not matter for the job I would be doing, if appointed. He promised to write, letting me know his decision. Two days later, which was the last Saturday in 1933, a letter arrived, telling me I had got the job, subject to a 12-months probationary period, and that I was to present myself for work on the following Monday.

My mother took me out and bought me a black jacket, pin-striped trousers and a trilby-hat, and on New Year's Day, 1934 I started work as an office-boy in the Claims Office of the Tramway and Omnibus Department in Congreve Street at a commencing salary of £45 a year. Everyone said I was a lucky young fellow to get a job offering the maximum security with the minimum of both ability and effort on my part, at a time of ever lengthening dole-queues and hunger-marches. I didn't enthuse about my good fortune, as I still hankered after a job in the wide open spaces, but nevertheless very soon became aware of the interesting and, in some instances, off-beat characters I found myself working with.

My boss, Mr. Jerromes, was the Claims Superintendent, a dark, middle-aged man of slightly below average stature, with astutely penetrating grey eyes. He sent for me shortly after my arrival, when he talked to me gravely about my future duties, stressing as he did so the confidential nature of the work, and that under no circumstances must I talk to anyone about anything I saw or heard in the course of my employment. I soon came to realise that this was a caveat with wider implications than at first appeared.

Mr. Jerromes was in the habit of disappearing at regular intervals during the earlier part of the day. Mid-morning he would vanish for 40 minutes or so, and again before lunch he would be away for another quite lengthy spell. His Mecca, I soon found, was the 'White Horse', just across the road from the office, but although everyone apparently knew of his whereabouts, it seemed to be something to which one was supposed to turn a blind eye.

Sometimes Mr. Baker, the General Manager, would come through on the dictograph, asking for Mr. Jerromes or, more spectacularly, he would appear in person, filling the doorway with his large, autocratic

Repairing the tram-track — a familiar scene in the tramway era.

presence. Having found our chief missing from his office, he would boom: "Where's Jerromes?" Someone would reply, platitudinously: "He's out of the office, Sir". "Find him!" Mr. Baker would bark, before stalking off majestically to his ballroom-sized office at the end of the corridor. It then became the responsibility of the senior man present to go across to the 'White Horse' to seek out Mr. Jerromes, who, when found, nursing a double whisky, would respond querulously: "How did you know I was here?"

*　*　*　*　*

My work in a public office was neither dull nor uninteresting. It brought me into contact with all manner of people, and the semi-legal role of the Claims Office made me aware for the first time of the functions of such dignitaries as the Town Clerk; the Chief Constable; the Prosecuting Solicitor and the City Coroner. The Department was in frequent touch with these exalted people and their staffs, as well as solicitors; trade union officials; insurers and insurance brokers, and Mr. Jerromes seemed to be on terms of easy familiarity with them all. The first inquest I ever attended was when, as an office-boy, I had to take some papers to Mr. Jerromes at the Coroner's Court, where he was representing the Department in connection with the death of some unfortunate 'bus accident victim. When I arrived, the inquest was about to start, and Mr. Jerromes said to me: "You might as well stay, Jones, it will be experience for you." It was indeed an experience for me, and it made me realise how much more of an experience it was — and a traumatic one at that — for some people. There can be few things more harrowing for anyone than, having lost a close relative under tragic and sometimes violent circumstances, than to have to relive all the gruesome details in the inhibiting surroundings of a Coroner's Court.

There was no such thing as Social Security benefit in those days, but anyone injured at work was, subject to certain conditions, eligible for payment of a pittance under the Workmen's Compensation Acts. Every Friday afternoon employees who had been victims of such accidents and were capable of walking would attend the office to collect their compensation and to be interviewed by a member of staff as to their progress. The waiting-room looked like a casualty clearing station, or a hospital out-patients' department, and splints, crutches, bandages and eye-shades were much in evidence. It was not just drivers and conductors who were injured at work. The majority of the victims were artisans, particularly the numerous workmen who helped maintain the hundreds of miles of tram-track then radiating in all directions from the centre of Birmingham. There were tar-pot men; oxy-acetylene cutters; grinders; welders; compressor-men; rammer-men; blacksmiths; plate-layers; navvies; gangers and paviors, and the injuries which they suffered at work were more varied than the trades which they practised.

Apart from all the usual chores associated with being an office-boy, such as ensuring that the incoming mail was dealt with promptly, answering the door and the telephone, filing the 'settled' claims, cleaning Mr. Jerromes' ink-well and seeing that he always had clean blotting-paper, fetching his newspaper and running errands, I had to do the occasional stint at typing, which entailed coming to terms with the three-banked keyboard of an antiquated Oliver typewriter. But I was at least spared one task: that of stoking the boss's fire. My friend, Frank, the General Manager's office-boy, had to go in at regular intervals to Mr. Baker's office and stoke up for him from a brightly shining scuttle on the hearth. Mr. Jerromes did not have a fire-grate in his office.

All callers had to be dealt with promptly, and as many of them were suffering pain or distress as a result of accidents, a polite, sympathetic approach was one of the prerequisites of the job. Sometimes, however, I would be told by a senior member of staff to get rid of a persistent or vexatious claimant for whom no payment was forthcoming or, no less difficult, to tell a claimant that the superintendent was out when he was, in fact, sitting in his office. Mr. Jerromes would sometimes tell me to cover up for him in this way, and I found the duty extremely difficult, being a poor liar, given to blushing and stammering at the critical moment, which I felt must surely proclaim my mendacity to the unwelcome caller.

Among those people I knew at work, I did not mind those who were forbidding, providing they were also in some way entertaining or 'different'. Unfortunately, Mr. Johnson, the Traffic Superintendent, who occupied a large office on the floor below where I worked, showed no quality to relieve the uniform severity of his personality. Sometimes I would be sent by Mr. Jerromes to deliver a file to Mr. Johnson, a duty I did not relish, but it was even worse when I was sent to recover papers from him, which usually entailed waiting nervously in front of his large desk while he looked for them, or otherwise being told by him, curtly, why I could not have them.

Mr. Johnson's chief role seemed to me to be to dispense a kind of rough justice to erring employees. The men under his jurisdiction were motormen, (the term always used officially to describe those who drove trams); 'bus drivers and conductors. Men graduated from conducting to driving, and the numbers of applicants for conducting jobs always exceeded the available vacancies, so that every day a cluster of 'hopefuls' would be awaiting the arrival of Mr. James, the Chief Clerk in the Traffic Department, whose job it was to choose suitable candidates for medical examination.

Suitability for the work entailed being of a minimum height of five foot seven inches and, as the vast majority of recruits were ex-regular army men, they were required to have unblemished military records. Once on the Department's pay-roll, employees were subjected to a form of discipline no less rigorous than that in the army. A conductor, for instance, who missed a fare would be hauled up before Mr. Johnson and after a verbal trouncing would probably be given three days suspension without pay; a driver or motorman who failed to pick up a passenger at a request-stop would be in serious trouble; and any employee proved to be in the slightest degree rude or offhand towards a passenger would quickly find himself at the end of a dole queue. On one occasion, following some kind of alleged 'incident' between a woman passenger and a conductor, resulting in a verbal exchange, the woman claimed, quite vehemently, that the conductor's parting shot was "Arse 'oles to you, ducks!" The man was promptly called over the coals, but from the outset he vigorously denied the allegation, saying that he would not, under any circumstances, say such a thing. No amount of interrogation moved him from his denial, and since there was no evidence to support the woman's claim, he had to be given the benefit of the doubt.

In view of Mr. Johnson's reputation, I was not altogether surprised to hear of an incident which had occurred a few years before I joined the Department, involving Johnson and his subordinate, Chief Inspector Cuttler. One day, so I was told, the usually quiet corridors of the council house rang to the sound of revolver shots. Clerks rushed into the Traffic Superintendent's office, from whence the shots had come,

Waiting for the tram, Saltley c. 1920

and discovered that Cuttler had shot Johnson. One of the clerks, Clem Tickle, grappled with the gun-man, while a second, Wilf Smith (a future General Manager of the Department), ran out to call a policeman.

Johnson was not seriously hurt, but Cuttler, a man of sixty, was charged with attempted murder and unlawful wounding. He was a popular man among the rank and file tram-men, and when they realised that, if convicted, he would go down for at least ten years, they organised a collection to pay for his defence. As a consequence they were able to brief Sir Norman Birkett, (later Lord Birkett), the most brilliant defence counsel of his day. At the trial Cuttler, showing no sign of remorse, claimed that, as he drew the gun, Johnson had rushed at him, when the gun went off by accident. When the prosecuting counsel asked Cuttler why he had drawn the revolver in the first place, he replied: "To force him to go along with me to the General Manager".

"What did you intend doing then?" he was asked, to which he replied: "If the Manager had backed up Johnson, I would have shot Johnson". "You were going to shoot him later?" interposed counsel, "Surely that was an amazing decision to make?" "He deserved it". responded Cuttler. Things looked bad for him.

Norman Birkett rose to his feet. After outlining Cuttler's eminent respectability, his long career and the feeling of frustration and injustice which had developed out of his relationship with Johnson, he asked the jury: "Can you really believe that Cuttler deliberately fired?" He went on to point out: "He failed to kill. He almost failed to wound, and yet he is a champion revolver shot. Would a brilliant marksman really shoot like this?" Cuttler, he added, had been amazingly honest to the court about his intentions. Why, therefore, not believe his story that what had happened was an accident?

The jury brought in a verdict of 'Not Guilty'. Cuttler walked free from the Victoria Law Courts, into Corporation Street, Birmingham, where a cluster of elated tram-men waited to carry him away, shoulder-high, to a place of celebration.

When I was young I often heard the story of the Cuttler and Johnson affair from people who had been on the premises at the time. No-one told it with more colour and gusto than Mr. Frederick George Hopton, a man in every way in sharp contrast with the forbidding Mr. Johnson. When it came to rotund good fellowship, Fred Hopton could outclass Falstaff himself. He was a big man, with a well-rounded figure and a rosy, well-rounded, shining face to match. I never knew as a youth exactly what his official job was, beyond the fact that he 'did something with figures'. Judging from his more obvious accomplishments, however, it was quite clear that he was a man of parts.

He edited the *Tramways Gazette*, for which he also wrote innumerable short stories; he was an able raconteur and after-dinner speaker, always ready with 'a few words' at the drop of a hat; he had green fingers and an uncanny knack of producing roses from his garden in almost every month of the year, so that he was rarely to be seen without a rose in his button-hole; every summer he organised a highly successful Baby Show at the Tramways Stadium at Kings Heath, sponsored by the impressively named "Birmingham Corporation Tramway and Omnibus Department Social, Athletic and Thrift Society"; and, in the best traditions of George Robey, who is said to have started life as a tram-man in Birmingham, Fred Hopton trod the boards as a stand-up comedian, under the stage name of 'Willit Raine'.

* * * * *

I discovered that there was more to working in the Claims Office than at first met the eye. There were books and law reports to read and new skills to be acquired. Medical reports needed to be understood, with or without the aid of a medical dictionary, and a knowledge of the law of evidence was necessary, together with the capacity to decide on the credibility of witnesses.

Some of the 'leading cases' had a relevance to the work we were doing. One such case, appearing in the law books as 'Polemis v. Furness, Withy & Co., (1921)', in which the supposed rule that a wrongdoer is only responsible for the natural and probable consequences of his act was rejected and established that, if negligence is proved, he is liable for the consequences, however unlikely. In this bizarre case, a stevedore, who was working for the charterers of a ship, negligently dropped a plank into the ship's hold, which was full of petrol vapour, and the whole ship was destroyed by fire. It was held that, although the consequences of this relatively minor act of negligence could not reasonably have been anticipated, the charterers were liable for the whole loss, amounting to nearly £200,000. This ruling, on the face of it, seemed at variance with the legal concept that the standard of conduct required at common law is that of the reasonable man — sometimes referred to by lawyers as 'the man on the Clapham omnibus'. But while the reasonable man could not, presumably, have anticipated the dire consquences of the plank being dropped, he would at least have anticipated some damage and taken steps to avoid the mishap in the first place.

A distinguished lawyer later defined the reasonable man as being "independent of the idiosyncrasies of the particular person whose conduct is in question". "Some persons" he continued "are by nature unduly timorous and imagine every path beset with lions; others, of more robust temperament, fail to foresee or nonchalantly disregard even the most obvious dangers. The reasonable man is presumed to be free both from over-apprehension and from over-confidence".

Resolving the question of who was to blame for an accident was often far from easy and the concept of the 'reasonable man' frequently became blurred. Claims men, in dealing with accident claims, were urged to ask themselves "Are we liable?" and if the answer to the question was "No", then no payment would be made. But often there was blame on both sides, which complicated the issue and, in many cases, resulted in long-drawn-out negotiations, sometimes terminating in law suits. The courts, I soon discovered, were unpredictable. Despite the cool logic they displayed from time to time, legal quibbles could cloud issues to the point of vexation, and only right at the end of proceedings, culminating in the judge's summing-up, was the outcome revealed. When a famous judge once declared: "The more I see of litigation, the more determined I am to keep out of it myself" he clearly knew what he was talking about.

Trams and trolley 'buses were propelled by electricity and it was not unusual for passengers to receive electric shocks from the fittings, particularly the hand-rails. The shocks were usually of a minor nature, but on one occasion, during a thunderstorm, a tramcar became 'alive' resulting in a number of passengers suffering burns. Mr. Jerromes, after consultation with the Town Clerk, decided to claim the defence of 'Act of God' with a view to avoiding liability. When this decision became known to the interested parties, there was a storm of a different kind, but the matter was eventually resolved by making ex gratia payments to the injured passengers.

On another occasion a motorman dropped dead at the controls of his tramcar, when a quick-witted passenger, who had seen what had happened, dashed to the front of the car and — despite the fact that he had no prior knowledge of the controls — brought the vehicle safely to a halt. The man whose prompt action had avoided what might have been a serious accident received a cheque in appreciation from a grateful management. He was also presented with a framed photograph of the platform and controls of a tramcar, which struck me at the time as being a somewhat prosaic gesture, although I kept my own counsel on the subject.

*   *   *   *   *

Photo: J. Willoughby Harrison

The Bull Ring c. 1928

CHAPTER V

Birmingham Between The Wars

.... every place is altered so,
There's hardly a single place I know;
And it fills my heart with grief and woe,
For I can't find Brummagem.

19th century song

Birmingham between the wars was still, as far as its buildings were concerned, predominantly Victorian, with a preponderance of red terracotta, which proliferated all around the town and into the inner suburbs. Pubs, libraries, offices, arcades, the Y.M.C.A., the telephone exchange, the Central Methodist Hall and the Victoria Law Courts were all built in red terracotta, as was the Smithfield Market, which was embellished with roundels of birds and animals in the same medium. Red terracotta has warmth and effulgence when clean, but in the grimy, smoke-laden atmosphere of the period its beauty had for long been hidden beneath successive layers of filth.

New Street's most distinguished building was King Edward VI's School. Impressively Gothic in style, it was designed by Sir Charles Barry — architect of the Houses of Parliament — with some assistance with the Gothic detail from A.W.N. Pugin, who designed Oscott College. Built in 1838 — the year of Birmingham's incorporation — the school survived until it was demolished in 1936. Nearby, at the corner of New Street and Stephenson Place, stood the Exchange, a strikingly resplendent structure, with a central tower, 110 feet high. During the 'twenties my father had an office several floors up in the Exchange, from where I would sometimes watch the traffic in the street below. Occasionally, Mr. Ike, a kindly man who worked with my father, would take me across to the sweet-shop on the opposite side of New Street to buy me jelly-babies.

The Exchange, Birmingham, from a Victorian print.

Victoria Square, then as now, was dominated by Yeoville Thomason's neo-classical council house, and the town hall, designed by Joseph Aloysius Hansom, who later gained immortality for himself by designing a cab which bore his name. Of the two concepts, perhaps the Hansom-cab — described by H.V. Morton as a sedan-chair slung between two huge wheels — was the more original, Birmingham town hall being a mere replica of a Roman temple. At the corner of New Street and Colmore Row was a large triangular building which, because of Galloway's chemist's shop, with windows facing Victoria Square being at the apex of the triangle, was always known as

New Street, Birmingham c. 1920
With acknowledgments to Birmingham Post and Mail

'Galloway's Corner'. The site had been formerly occupied by Christ Church, which was demolished in 1899, hence the name of Christ Church Passage, running between New Street and Waterloo Street.

Mason College in Edmund Street was built by Josiah Mason, a poor boy from Kidderminster, who made a vast fortune in Birmingham out of split-rings, steel-pens and electro-plating. The college, which provided new educational opportunities, particularly in the sciences, became the nucleus of Birmingham University, which was opened at Edgbaston

Paradise Street, Birmingham 1938, showing a L.M.S. Railway dray-horse.
Reproduced by permission of Birmingham Central Library
Local Studies Department.

in 1909. Across the road from Mason College stood the massive, four-square free library, with its splendidly impressive interior, a monument to the cultural aspirations of the Victorians and their belief in the efficacy of self-help. Next door to the free library, on the corner of Ratcliffe Place and Paradise Street, was the Birmingham and Midland Institute and the School of Music.

The most striking as well as the most interesting building in Paradise Street was Queen's College Chambers, (since reduced to a mere façade), where, in 1828, W. Sands Cox, a Birmingham surgeon, had founded a School of Medicine and Surgery. Within the college there were also faculties in Theology and the Arts, and behind the building, only to be seen from Swallow Street, there was a little mortuary, belonging to the School of Medicine and Surgery, and a chapel, built for the use of the theological students. In 1892 the School was absorbed

". . . a bearded woodman, axe in hand and dog at his side, gazing solemnly across the traffic."

Reproduced by permission of Birmingham Central Library, Local Studies Department.

by Mason's College and became, for a while, the Medical Faculty of the University before its establishment at Edgbaston.

No. 1, Easy Row was the shop of Bellamy and Wakefield, chemists, famous for over a century for their skill in charming away warts. Nearby was the Woodman Inn, over the entrance of which was its impressive figure of a bearded woodman, axe in hand and dog at his side, gazing solemnly across the traffic. On the steep cobbled slope of

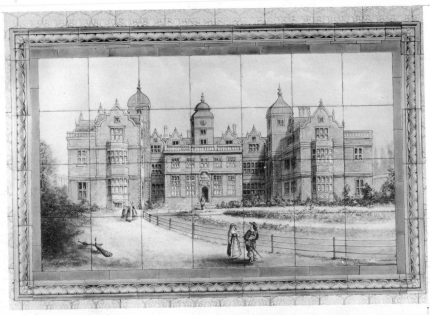

Wall tiles from the interior of the Woodman Inn in Easy Row.
Reproduced by permission of Birmingham Central Library,
Local Studies Department.

Hill Street, c. 1935, showing roof of New Street Station in the background.

Suffolk Street — always a trial of strength for the dray-horses from the nearby railway depot — stood the terracotta Municipal Technical School, and lower down the hill, at the corner of Navigation Street, was a taxidermist's shop, its windows always stocked with a variety of skins of poor, ill-fated birds and animals, victims of storm and shot, perpetuated beyond death by the taxidermist's art.

Birmingham had several distinctive 'quarters'. The jewellery quarter was around Hockley and centering on St. Paul's Church and Square. Nearby, in Frederick Street, was the house where Washington Irving, the American writer, wrote 'Rip Van Winkle', which, according to the legend, was dashed off by candle-light in the course of one night. The gunsmiths were mainly to be found at the back of the General Hospital, in Loveday Street and along Steelhouse Lane. I remember the hue and cry when, at the time of Italy's unwarranted attack on

Abyssinia in 1935, it was claimed that a gunsmith in Steelhouse Lane was supplying dumdum bullets to the Italians. A lesser-known 'quarter' was that of the printers, situated in and around Cornwall Steet, Church Street and Great Charles Street.

In those days Birmingham was well provided with theatres and music-halls. There was the Theatre Royal in New Street, associated with many famous theatrical names, including those of Henry Irving, Ivor Novello, Sybil Thorndike and Noel Coward. In Broad Street stood the Prince of Wales Theatre, (later to be a victim of German bombing), and in Station Street Barry Jackson's somewhat cramped Repertory Theatre was producing seasons of first-class plays. Birmingham audiences were reputed to be critical, and for that reason plays were often given their premières in the town, and if well received and reviewed they were then considered to be a 'safe bet' for the West End stage.

Music-hall entertainment was still alive and kicking at the Hippodrome and the Empire, both in Hurst Street, at the Grand Theatre in Corporation Street, opposite the Old Square, later converted into the Casino Dance Hall, and at the Aston Hippodrome in High Street, Aston. The Grand Theatre was well named, having as it did a splendid marble staircase, leading to the grand and upper circles. It was decorated in cream and gold, with its seats upholstered in crimson. I remember going there twice as a child, once to see and hear Jack Hylton's Band, and again when I was about twelve to see a revue, on which occasion I remember noticing for the first time as I watched the chorus doing their dance routine that girls' legs could be very attractive. The Grand closed in 1933. Aston Hippodrome was considered to be somewhat 'down market', but it was in the nature of a spring-board for many up-and-coming artists, who were later to appear top of the bill at other halls. Just across the road from the Aston Hippodrome the 'Barton's Arms' pub with its stained glass windows, mahogany fittings and tiled staircase did much to recapture the atmosphere of that era around the turn-of-the-century which was music-hall's high noon.

To savour the hurly-burly of Birmingham life, no better place could be found than the Bull Ring, little changed in appearance then from when David Cox, the Birmingham-born painter depicted it early in the nineteenth century. Walking down the Bull Ring from High Street, beside the steps leading to the old market hall, and beyond, towards the church, the cries of the barrow-boys would fill the air. Their kerb-

A turn-of-the-century photograph of the Grand Theatre, Corporation Street, known originally as the New Theatre. It closed its doors for the last time in 1933.

Photo by Thomas Lewis   *Reproduced by permission of Birmingham Central Library, Local Studies Department*

side barrows were laden with pyramids of apples, plums and tomatoes, always with the best ones displayed to advantage and some dubious ones sometimes secreted at the back of the barrow for slipping into the bags of unsuspecting customers.

Down the middle of the wide expanse of the Bull Ring the canvas-covered market-stalls were set up several times a week for the sale of poultry, rabbits, plants, flowers and shrubs. Lower down and in front of the church was Nelson's statue and 'Speaker's Corner'. The statue was paid for by public subscription and unveiled in 1809, its purpose being, according to a contemporary account, to enable the people of

Six Ways Erdington in 1926, when it acquired its gyratory island — the first in England outside London.

Birmingham to honour the memory of 'the saviour of the silver-coasted isle'. At 'Speaker's Corner' orators had the opportunity to air their views, however extreme short of being treasonable. Sometimes a speaker would so incense his audience with his way-out views that he would have to retreat to the sanctuary of the underground public lavatories nearby, and lock himself in one of them for a 'cooling off' period.

* * * * *

Birmingham during the inter-war years was expanding and absorbing villages and hamlets in the countryside around its perimeter. The city was ringed with new estates which sprang up at Kingstanding, Pype Hayes, Glebe Farm, Fox Hollies, Billesley, Weoley Castle and Quinton. During the 20 years from 1919 to the renewed outbreak of war in 1939, over 50,000 municipal houses were built in Greater Birmingham.

Because of their speed and mobility, 'buses rather than trams and trolley 'buses were used increasingly in these outlying areas, a fact which was reflected in the changing designation of the transport undertaking. In 1927 the Birmingham Corporation Tramways became the Birmingham Corporation Tramway and Omnibus Department, and ten years later it changed its name again to Birmingham City Transport. One 'bus service which caught the public imagination was the 'Outer Circle', which commenced operation in April, 1926. "See Birmingham's charming suburbs by 'bus — 25 miles for 15 pence" said the introductory leaflet, and a surprising number of people responded to the suggestion.

One did not have to go so far to pick blackberries or hear the skylark in those days, and from the vantage point of the upper deck of a solid-tyred 'bus encircling the city's outskirts, many of the roads traversed bore a distinct resemblance to country lanes. The popular name for the Outer Circle was the 'love 'bus' on account of its attraction for courting couples. In an era when very few young people had cars, they would spend a pleasant Sunday afternoon — sharing a double seat and holding hands — as they did the round journey, in many instances through places previously unfamiliar to them.

PASSENGER & COMMERCIAL
MOTOR VEHICL

THE famous ran
Vehicles extens
and successfully c
ted by leading Mun
Authorities at Hom
Overseas.

*Illustrated : One
large fleet of
Buses owned and
ted by the Birm
Corporation.*

Apply for full particulars and specifi
of all latest Models, embodying striki
features of construction and design.

**PASSENGER
VEHICLES**
21-68 Seaters

THE ASSOCIATED EQUIPMENT CO. LTD.
5 - 8, CAROLINE STREET, BIRMINGHAM.
'*Phone: Central* 8383-4. *Wires:"Vangastow, Birmingham."*

*Head Office and Works:
Windmill Lane, Southall,
MIDDLESEX.*

**GOOD
VEHICL**
2-6 Ton

A 1928 advertisement showing a typical Birmingham Bus of the period.

Birmingham acquired, in 1920, its own shop-window on the world.
The British Industries Fair, held annually at Castle Bromwich, was
inaugurated to exhibit the vast range of the city's products, including
brassware, ironmongery, transport, building material, heating and
cooking appliances and heavy engineering goods. Organised by the
Birmingham Chamber of Commerce, the fair was described in the 1932
City Handbook as "the largest trade exhibition ever seen in this

The British Industries Fair at Castle Bromwich, which spanned 9½ acres, was a business fair where buyers and sellers could meet. The open land alongside it, now occupied by the Castle Vale Estate, was once Castle Bromwich Aerodrome. Previously it had been used for demonstration flights by B.C. Hucks in a Bleriot monoplane in 1911.

country, and the Castle Bromwich buildings probably constitute the largest one-storey permanent exhibition hall in the world". For two weeks each year the little railway station at Castle Bromwich, built by the Midland Railway Company in 1842, assumed the important role of catering for large numbers of visitors to the fair, including Royal ones, necessitating the unrolling of the red carpet from time to time.

Beyond the site of the British Industries Fair, which lay in the valley of the River Tame, rose the sharp mound of Castle Bromwich's 'motte and bailey', where once stood the castle which defended the ancient ford across the river below it. The climb to Castle Bromwich village

Christ Church, Aldridge Road Junction, Perry Barr 1933

Reproduced by permission of Birmingham Central Library, Local Studies Department.

was very beautiful in those days, by way of a well-wooded road, carrying a traffic-sign warning: 'Bends for one-third of a mile'. At the top of the hill the 'Queen Anne' parish church, cocooned amid its ancient yews, was a convenient spot for the cyclist to stop, mop his brow and walk across the churchyard to the high wall and the gateway leading to Castle Bromwich Hall, still then occupied as a stately home by the Dowager Countess of Bradford. On either side of the iron gates were little alcoves, built into the wall, known as 'footman's porches', where flunkeys once stood to hand out bibles and prayer-books to the occupants of the hall, as they passed through the gates on their way to church.

* * * * *

CHAPTER VI

Holidays

*"August Bank Holiday. A tune on an ice-cream
cornet. A slap of sea and a tickle of sand.
A fanfare of sunshades opening. A wince and whinny
of bathers dancing into deceptive waters.
A tuck of dresses. A rolling of trousers."*

Dylan Thomas

HOLIDAYS WERE not equated with trips to far-away places. They generally merely meant a temporary cessation of the common round, when one had more time for chosen activities close at hand. I cannot remember even the suggestion of a seaside holiday between 1924, when we went to Lowestoft, and 1932, when we had a week at Margate. Some of our holidays, however, were spent in visiting relatives in various parts of the country, including London, Cardiff, Cirencester and North Wales.

Visits to London, if made by rail, posed the question: L.M.S. or G.W.R? The L.M.S. run from New Street to Euston by way of Coventry and Rugby, was the shorter route. By G.W.R. from Snow Hill to Paddington was a slower, more devious journey, which led to the quip that G.W.R. stood for "Great Way Round". But either way, in those memorable days of steam, there were attractions for the railway connoisseurs, whether in the green liveries of the Great Western route or the red of the London, Midland and Scottish, dominated in the inter-war years by their magnificent 'Royal Scots'.

Our journey to London usually started from beneath the huge steel and glass arched roof of New Street Station which, when built in 1853, was the largest station in England. Steaming out from there, past countless factories and chimney-stacks, miles of sidings and endless rows of trucks, beyond the little urban homes into the leafy middle-English countryside, we were, just two hours later, entering the

Photo: J. Willoughby Harrison

New Street Station c. 1928

THE ENTRANCE TO EUSTON STATION. L M S

streets of the Metropolis, through the Doric arch of Euston's old station.

Our journey to Margate in 1932 was made by rail, necessitating changing stations at London, in the course of which we broke our journey long enough to visit the Tate Gallery in Millbank. I remember this vividly because of the impact Stanley Spencer's 'Resurrection' made on my youthful mind. Was the artist to be taken seriously with his mundane little figures, rising from their graves on Judgment Day, I wondered, or was he enjoying a sly joke at the expense of the viewer?

At Margate my father made a number of pencil sketches, my mother read a novel by Warwick Deeping and when I wasn't eyeing the bathing-belles or enjoying the innuendo of the comic post-cards along the front I dabbled at marine biology by scouring the shore for shells, which I attempted to classify after my return home. My father later used his sketches, when he painted a seascape in oils, which, to my untutored eye, seemed to capture the mood of a summer's evening

Top: Margate in the 'thirties.   Bottom: Calais with icecream seller in foreground
Photos: Wilfred M. Jones

beside the sea. One sunny day we rode on the upper-deck of an open-topped tramcar from Margate to Broadstairs, through fields of golden corn, waving in the breeze, beneath a July sky and brightened to the intensity of a Van Gogh canvas by a profusion of crimson poppies.

For several successive years after that we went away for holidays at the seaside, which may have been due to the fact that, early in 1933, my father acquired a Morris 10 h.p. saloon, having sold the Morgan Runabout early in the Depression, some years previously. Foreign travel, except for the well-to-do, was rare in those days, but on a second visit to Margate I decided that, as no passport was required, I would like to go for a day trip to Calais. My parents, thinking perhaps that France was no place for a callow youth to go alone, decided to go, too. And so it was that they had their one and only trip abroad, and I had a tiny foretaste of foreign travel, of which, in a few years time, I was to have a surfeit.

From the deck of the s.s. *Royal Sovereign*, so soon to achieve its finest hour at the evacuation of the British Expeditionary Force from Dunkirk, we compared the respective scenic merits of Cap Gris Nez and the White Cliffs of Dover from mid-channel, and on arrival in Calais, strolled through the cobbled streets, admired Rodin's 'Les Bourgeois de Calais', sampled the town's vin rouge and gave voice to our rusty and unused school French to the amusement if not the understanding of one or two of the natives.

* * * * *

CHAPTER VII

"How is the Empire?"

B Y 1935, despite two-and-a-half million unemployed, there were glimmers of light in the economic gloom which had prevailed for the previous five years. Many people felt that the Depression was over, and since the gathering war-clouds had not yet become too ominous, some measure of optimism prevailed at the prospect of what appeared to be a brighter future. The time did not seem to be entirely inappropriate for a celebration, and the Silver Jubilee of King George V. was as good a reason as any for having one, particularly when it was made known that the event was to take place in May, the traditional month for merry-making in the English calendar.

The Royal Family, in my early childhood, consisted of remote beings, seen only on rare occasions, if at all, whose likenesses were known mainly through newspaper photographs. I remember, once, having a fleeting glimpse of the Prince of Wales, as he sped along Hagley Road in a large, open touring-car and, on another occasion, when in Kensington High Street with my mother and an aunt, spotting a green Daimler limousine of some distinction, before recognising the occupant to be of even greater distinction. "Look!" I said, nudging my mother: "It's Queen Mary". But I had never seen the King, who was always more than a King. He was the King-Emperor, a fact which was proclaimed on the coin of the realm in the truncated and cryptic words: GEORGIVS V. DEI. GRA. BRITT. OMN. REX FID. DEF. IND. IMP., which, my mother explained to me, meant that he was not only King and Defender of the Faith, but that he was also Emperor of India, the exalted role which had been held by his father, Edward VII, Queen Victoria — George V's grandmother — having been proclaimed Empress of India at Delhi in 1877.

Postcard commemorating the year of the three Kings.

At Christmas, 1932, the King-Emperor's voice had been heard for the first time on the wireless. "Through one of the marvels of modern science" he proclaimed across the ether "I am enabled, this Christmas Day, to speak to all my peoples throughout the Empire . . ." In an unaffected, slightly guttural voice he spoke for several minutes, conveying a message of warmth and kindness to all his subjects everywhere. The dramatic impact of the broadcast gave a new lustre to the monarchy, and for each succeeding Christmas of his reign, the King-Emperor sent a similar message of paternal goodwill over the air so that, as the Jubilee approached, a considerable amount of spontaneous warmth was felt for the old man whose reign had spanned 25 years of turbulent history.

Jubilee Day, the 6th May, 1935, was a national holiday. It was a fine, warm day, and the working population enjoyed having a Monday off which it would not otherwise have had. For one day there was a return to Merrie England. Cities, towns and villages up and down the land were colourfully and lavishly decorated and illuminated; there were street parties for the children; ox-roastings; and all manner of displays and parades. In Sutton Park there was maypole dancing and morris dancing; 3,000 children were given free teas in marquees; the Crystal Palace fair, like Punch and Judy and the boats at Blackroot Pool, did a roaring trade; and at night there was a spectacular firework display at Holly Knoll, the centre-piece of which was a huge, pyrotechnic portrait of the King on the hill-side, facing the Meadow Platt. Beyond the Park's confines, on Maney Hill, the Scouts lit a beacon, one of 2,000 which were lit on hills all around the country, and the streets of Sutton Coldfield were thronged with visitors until a late hour, enjoying the decorations beneath the light of the town's brilliant illuminations.

There were surprisingly few protests over the expenditure of so much money at a time of national stringency, and we heard afterwards that the old gentleman in whose honour the celebration was enacted, on seeing the demonstrations of public acclaim in the Capital, had remarked to his consort: "I'd no idea they felt like that about me. I am beginning to think they just really like me for myself".

In January, 1936, the King-Emperor died, and on the day following his death, Mr. Baldwin, the Prime Minister, speaking on the wireless, claimed that the dying monarch, in his last conscious moments, had asked his secretary: "How is the Empire?" "All is well, Sir, with the Empire", replied the secretary, and the King-Emperor had smiled, and relapsed into unconsciousness. His successor, Edward VIII, reigned for only 325 days and was never crowned. Because of his love for Mrs. Simpson, an American divorcee, and on account of the constitutional crisis arising out of that liaison, he abdicated in favour of his younger brother, who became George VI; and so it came about that the year 1936 spanned three reigns.

* * * * *

CHAPTER VIII

"Doing the Lambeth Walk"

M USIC WAS ALWAYS very much a part of the life of my childhood home. My mother, as a young girl, had taught herself to play the piano, and my father had a good baritone voice and a modest repertoire of ballads. When we visited friends, or entertained them at home, he was often asked to sing, and when he did so my mother would accompany him on the piano. My father also had a banjo, which he played moderately well, and from my early childhood we had a gramophone, by means of which I became familiar with much classical and light-classical music. But it was the wireless which made the greatest musical impact upon our household. It was the means by which melody could be dispensed at the touch of a button. I remember the joy of first hearing Beethoven's Fifth Symphony when listening to 'the Proms' on the wireless in 1936. By this time the quality of receiving sets had improved immeasurably. Over the years my father, working from blueprints and through the medium of 'superhet' valves, had made a series of sets, each one better than its predecessor. His efforts culminated in one with a huge speaker, hidden behind a fretwork front in the shape of a Gothic window, backed by gold-lace curtain material. The music emanating from this set was of a high quality, and in a television-less age, 'listening to the wireless' became a daily pleasure, far removed from the frustrations of the 'cat's whisker' era of a decade earlier.

Some of the programmes I listened to did not appeal to my father, and 'crooners' were his particular *bête noire*. They were often the star turns of one or other of the numerous dance-orchestras which supplied late-night music on the air. Roy Fox, Jack Payne, Henry Hall, Ambrose, Harry Roy and all the other top-liners each had their vocalists, whose laments over lost love and the state of their hearts sometimes caused my father's annoyance to erupt. "Emasculated buggers!" he would snap. "If ever Hitler listens to this, he'll think we're decadent!"

Not all the melodies of the period were on the theme of love, lost or otherwise. Some of them reflected the mood of the Depression. Tin Pan Alley was nothing if not enterprising. There was 'Buddy, can you spare a Dime?', 'Ain't it Grand to be Bloomin' well Dead!' 'Underneath the Arches' and a sad but catchy little tune, lamenting the fact that there was:

> *No more money in the Bank!*
> *No cute baby you can spank!*
> *What's to do about it?*
> *Let's put out the lights and go to sleep!*

With the advancing decade and the receding Depression, the mood changed, with a corresponding shift of emphasis in the new lyrics. This changing mood was reflected in the crooning voice of Bing Crosby, of whom it was said he sang the way he did because of a defect in his vocal chords, so earning for himself in the fullness of time the nickname of 'the old groaner'. Crosby singing 'Love in Bloom' moaned of a love uninhibited by the state of the economy, and a year or so later the shortening dole queues were commemorated by 'Whistle While you Work!', one of the hit-tunes from Walt Disney's 'Snow White and the Seven Dwarfs'.

Perhaps no melody reflected more truly the happier mood of the era than the 'Lambeth Walk', first sung by Lupino Lane in 'Me and my Girl' at the Chelsea Palace late in 1937. At about that time I started attending a beginners' class in ballroom dancing at St. Peter's Church Hall, Maney, run by Madame Amies from Lozells. She was a tall lady of indeterminate age, (she had, I discovered later, been running her dancing school with her husband since 1902), and her accomplished skill in imparting a modicum of her own elegance and ease of movement to her pupils was immensely reassuring to gauche ones like me.

Beneath a large painting of the Via Dolorosa, I struggled with the intricacies of the quickstep, the slow foxtrot, the waltz, the tango, the rumba, the Palais Glide and the St. Bernard's Waltz. Within a comparatively short time I found, to my considerable surprise, that — like most of the other pupils — I could complete the circuit of the hall without trampling on my partner's feet, simultaneously with making desultory attempts at conversation with her.

One week we were introduced to a new dance, just created for the purpose of translating the melody of the 'Lambeth Walk' into lively movement, and soon we had all mastered its swaggering, Devil-may-care, 'thumbs-up' motions. To the words:

> Any time you're Lambeth way,
>   Any evening, any day,
> You'll find us all doin' the Lambeth Walk.
>   Ev'ry little Lambeth gal,
> With her little Lambeth pal,
>   You'll find 'em all doin' the Lambeth Walk.
>
> Ev'rything free and easy,
>   Do as you darn well pleasey,
> Why don't you make your way there,
>   Go there, stay there,
> Once you get down Lambeth way,
>   Ev'ry evening, ev'ry day,
> You'll find yourself doin' the Lambeth Walk.

unmindful of any incongruity, we captured something of the free and easy spirit attributed to the somewhat improbable gals and pals down Lambeth Way.

*   *   *   *   *

The Munich crisis 1938
Congreve Street and Edmund Street junction, sandbagged and ready for the worst.
Photo: E.H. Sargeant

CHAPTER IX

Trouble in a Faraway Country

THAT WHICH, in contemporary judgment, passes for collective wisdom often, in the light of history, turns out to be collective folly. Collective folly in the 'thirties played its part in the inexorable drift towards total war, but it was the inability of leaders everywhere to come to terms with the world's economic crisis which impinged most upon people's awareness. After all, war, as yet, was only a threat, and although its implications were graphically depicted in the film adaptation of H.G. Wells' 'The Shape of Things to Come', which was a great box-office success in the mid-'thirties, the symptoms of economic disorder were more of a reality than a mere threat.

Among the curious public figures of the period, Stanley Baldwin is remembered less for his ability as Prime Minister, or for his political acumen, than as a stolid, pipe-smoking student of the classics, who claimed that, during free time between electioneering speeches, he would read Homer and Horace and, as a consequence, even if defeated, he could say that he had passed through the fire, but that the smell of burning was not on his garments.

There was another side to Baldwin, too, who spoke with obvious emotion about his own vision of England. He was moved to eulogise the wild anemones in the April woods; the tinkle of the hammer on the anvil in the country smithy and the sound of the corncrake on a dewy morning. Most evocative, perhaps, were his words upon his beloved Bewdley, and his early recollection of looking up the river from the bridge there, 'into that mysterious and romantic land of Shropshire . . . watching the smoke of the train running along the little railway, through places bearing names like Wyre Forest, Cleobury Mortimer, Neen Sollars and Tenbury — names steeped in romance and redolent of the springtime of an England long ago passed, but whose heritage is ours'. Strong stuff this, and to a lover of the English countryside like myself, intelligible in a way that no political platitudes could be. The Englishman, according to Baldwin, was made for a time of crisis, and for a time of emergency. He was, Baldwin declared: '. . . . serene in difficulties and supreme in staying power'. The testing time for his compatriots was nearer than he probably realised.

In 1937 'honest Stan Baldwin' assumed the title of Earl Baldwin of Bewdley and was succeeded by Neville Chamberlain as Prime Minister. All through the decade the rumblings of approaching war grew more ominous. Italy's attack on Abyssinia, leading to the conquest of that unfortunate country within the year, was followed by the Spanish Civil War, during which the 'blueprint' bombing of the Basque town of Guernica by German 'planes, in support of General Franco, the commander of the insurgents, gave a foretaste of the aerial horrors which were so soon to become commonplace. There was war in the Far East, and in Germany, following Adolf Hitler's rise to power a few years earlier, there were frequent reminders of his insatiable territorial demands. All in all, the future looked black.

The year 1938 was, perhaps, more traumatic than its predecessors. In early March, Hitler seized Austria, thereby achieving at a stroke his long-term goal of 'Anschluss', or union between Germany and Austria. He then turned his propaganda machine on to the alleged hardships of the Sudeten German minority in Czechoslovakia. Tension increased, culminating in September in the last-ditch efforts by Britain and France to avert war, and the final meeting at Munich between Hitler, Mussolini, Daladier, the French Premier, and Neville Chamberlain, resulting in the Czech Sudetenland being ceded to Germany.

Chamberlain returned in triumph from Germany, armed with a 'scrap of paper' promising 'Peace in our time!' Relief and a feeling of having been reprieved was widespread, and not many people were unduly worried about the misfortunes of the Czechs, or the fate of their now truncated country. One journalist asked: "Why has Chamberlain 'turned all four cheeks' to Hitler?" and a European commentator described Neville Chamberlain as "a narrow-minded businessman from Birmingham with an instinctive English, surburban dislike of foreigners". Chamberlain was certainly from Birmingham — he was a son of the great Joseph Chamberlain, remembered affectionately in

The Aftermath "Chamberlain the Peacemaker" — at the News Cinema, High Street, Birmingham.

Photo: E.H. Sargeant

the town for all he had done to improve the living conditions of its inhabitants during his term of office as mayor in the late nineteenth century. The commentator may have based his judgment of Neville Chamberlain on a broadcast by him during the Czech crisis: "How horrible, fantastic, incredible it is" he said "that we should be digging trenches and trying on gas-masks here because of a quarrel in a faraway country between people of whom we know nothing". But whatever the man in the street may have thought of Chamberlain, it was generally accepted that Czechoslovakia *was* a faraway country, and no-one knew how we could have helped her people.

* * * * *

My guide, philosopher and friend was Ernie Bowater, whose knowledge of all things military seemed to be unlimited
—see page 99

CHAPTER X

1939

*"History is little more than
the register of the crimes, follies
and misfortunes of mankind".*

Edward Gibbon

NEW YEAR, 1939 brought no immediate threat of war, and there seemed to be a reasonable prospect of life continuing normally throughout the year. After all, had not Mr. Chamberlain brought us back from the brink only a few months earlier, when he had offered us the glittering prospect of 'Peace in our time'? For those of us who were young, life stretched invitingly ahead, with no real inkling of the great disruption which was so close at hand. The things we talked about were often those far removed from the international situation, sex and money being two evergreen subjects of conversation. Marriage, as Bernard Shaw had pointed out, is popular because it combines the maximum of temptation with the maximum of opportunity, and some of my near contemporaries at work were already married. The going must have been hard for them, for earnings in the local government service were notoriously low. It was the price one had to pay for security and the knowledge that, subject to conforming to certain standards of probity, one was hardly likely to end up in a dole queue. My own salary in 1939 was £105 a year.

Harold, a clerk in the Permanent Way Department, said in his laconic way: "Marriage is out as far as I'm concerned — I'm not prepared to change my tailor!" I could see what he meant, for he was always impeccably dressed. I did not have a tailor in Harold's sense of the word, for I usually bought my suits off the peg at the Thirty-five Shilling Tailors in Birmingham's High Street, my attitude to money having been influenced by my mother's frugality and good housekeeping habits rather than by my father's more casual attitude, preferring, as he did, to let the future take care of itself.

On 30th January, Hitler, in a bellicose speech, demanded the return of those colonies lost to Germany following the Great War, and on 15th March, without the Czechs having fired a shot in their own defence, the German armies marched into Prague, thus subjugating the whole of that ill-fated country. A week later, following a German ultimatum to Lithuania to surrender the town of Memel — detached from Germany under the Treaty of Versailles in 1919 — the Lithuanians gave way, and Memel was re-incorporated in Germany. The British Government denounced Hitler and saw fit to guarantee the sovereignty of Greece, Rumania and Poland.

At Easter I went on a walking holiday in Shropshire with my friend, Vic Cox, who shared my enjoyment of books and the outdoor life, and for whom the trip was the opportunity to do some water-colour sketching. For me, lacking Vic's artistic talent, it was a chance to observe nature, make notes and enjoy the beauty of the Shropshire hills. We set out on the morning of Good Friday to take the train from Snow Hill Station to Shrewsbury. The news had just broken of Italy's invasion of the tiny Kingdom of Albania, and because it was a holiday and more people had time to consider such things, everyone we met on the journey seemed to be talking about that pint-sized country's predicament. It soon became apparent, however, that a lot of them had no idea where Albania was.

On reaching Shrewsbury, Vic and I took a 'bus to Church Stretton, from whence we set out along the Carding-mill Valley for the heights of the Long Mynd. Soon, with the wild call-note of the curlew ringing in our ears and a clear sky overhead, our gloomy forebodings of impending war were temporarily dispelled. For the first night of our holidays we gained a friendly roof over our heads at Wentnor, a tiny village overshadowed by the Long Mynd ridge, and for the three following days we wandered through the peaceful and almost traffic-free by-ways of Shropshire, reaching Ludlow by the afternoon of Easter Monday. Despite aching feet, we rounded off our holiday by going to a dance at Ludlow town-hall before returning home the next day.

*   *   *   *   *

Undeterred by the gathering storm, the holiday promoters produced their usual spring crop of brochures. The 'big four' railway companies — the Great Western; the London, Midland and Scottish: the London and North Eastern and the Southern Railway Companies — each published their Holiday Guides for 1939. The particular attractions of waiting until September, one brochure pointed out, were that seas were warmer, accommodation cheaper and travel more comfortable due to trains being less crowded. Other promoters spelt out the pleasures of foreign travel, exemplified by a nine-day visit to Belgium for under five pounds, or a thirteen-day coach tour of the Riviera, 'all in' for £12.

With Hitler's tirades — now directed against Poland — reaching a crescendo of fury as the year passed its zenith, the dog-days of an uneasy summer slipped by. I listened to the various nostrums being peddled around, and wondered what particular 'ism' could bring Europe back from the brink now. There seemed to be no way out of the situation.

My guide, philosopher and friend was Ernie Bowater, whose knowledge of all things military seemed to be unlimited. He was one of four claims inspectors I worked with, whose job it was to visit and interview claimants in their own homes and to chase 'fare dodgers' and other defaulters. Because they wore blue serge uniforms with gold braid I called them, somewhat irreverently, 'admirals in the Swiss navy'. Ernie's uniform tunic was bedecked with campaign ribbons, and we who were privileged to know him did not doubt for one moment that he had had a distinguished and colourful military career in the Great War. We did, however, sometimes wonder if some of his more lurid tales were a trifle exaggerated, particularly as his cheerful rotundity of form did not seem to be designed for heroics.

Ernie's yarn about escaping from captivity while a prisoner of the Turks in the Dardanelles, which entailed cutting the throat of a sleeping sentry in the middle of the night, was told by him with particular gusto, and no-one had the nerve to suggest that he might have been spoofing. Subsequent events, however, did much to enhance his military reputation, for within weeks of the Home Guard being formed in 1940, we heard that he had become a battalion commander with the rank of lieutenant-colonel.

"The balloon will go up as soon as they've got the harvest in" said Ernie, with an air of unaccustomed gravity, and he gave me a bit of

The Council House extension, Congreve Street, which shows the office where I started work on New Year's Day, 1934 — as an office boy at a commencing salary of £45 a year

advice: "Whatever you do, Doug, don't go in the infantry" he said. It was advice I was prepared to listen to, for I had read a good many books about the Great War and my vicarious knowledge of it had been coloured by innumerable yarns and anecdotes from old soldiers who had survived its horrors. Life in the infantry, according to Ernie, was altogether too hazardous, and he suggested that I chose either the Medical Corps, the Engineers or the Ordnance Corps when the time came.

*　*　*　*　*

I didn't spend all my waking hours contemplating Europe's dilemma. I had both the time and the inclination to do some of those things appropriate to my age and taste. I courted a girl or two; I swam in Sutton Park; I went camping and I cycled to North Wales along roads not yet cluttered with motor traffic, and over mountain tracks even less

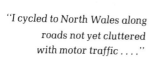

"I cycled to North Wales along roads not yet cluttered with motor traffic . . . ."

"... Coventry, despite its industrial growth, retained the architectural heritage of a medieval city, so soon to be reduced to rubble by German bombs."

cluttered, and designated 'dangerous but passable'. Nearer home I explored by bike many of the towns and villages within easy cycling distance of Sutton Coldfield, including Tamworth, Lichfield, Coventry and Coleshill.

Tamworth, the ancient capital of Mercia, and Lichfield with the three-spired splendour of its cathedral, vied with each other in historic interest, while Coventry, despite its industrial growth, retained the architectural heritage of a medieval city, so soon to be reduced to rubble by German bombs. For 'atmosphere' and ease of access the old town of Coleshill had much to offer, despite the fact that, having the steepest High Street in the whole of Warwickshire, it was something of a cyclists' nightmare. The Swan Hotel, the old coaching house at the top of the High Street was a reminder of the time when the coachman's horn reverberated through the town, and the tired and thirsty traveller was grateful for having reached a place where he had the choice of twenty-eight inns at which to slake his thirst.

Of all the villages within easy reach of home, Middleton — half way between Sutton and Tamworth — was my favourite. In those days church-doors were always open to visitors, and the attraction of Middleton's Norman church was reflected in the number of entries in the Visitors' Book. The recurring name among the church memorials was that of Willoughby, whose family had formerly lived at nearby Middleton Hall. Close to the altar I discovered a large, somewhat neglected plaque, commemorating Francis Willoughby, the naturalist son of Sir Francis and Lady Cassandra Willoughby, of whom it was said that he was so engrossed in the pursuit of scientific knowledge that he studied a flea for three months by allowing it to suck a daily draught of blood from his hand. During his short life in the seventeenth century, Willoughby made a lasting name for himself in collaboration with John Ray, a blacksmith's son from Essex, a Fellow of Trinity College, Cambridge, and sometimes called 'the father of English natural history'. Willoughby's book, 'Ornithology', published posthumously, was claimed to be the first illustrated bird book ever written.

*   *   *   *   *

I was sitting in the office on the morning of Friday, 1st September, when a newsboy ran along Congreve Street with a special edition of the *Despatch*. "Poland invaded!" he shouted, whereupon Linda, the typist, became hysterical, effectively drowning with an emotional outburst the strident calls of the news-vendor. At lunchtime, taking my customary walk around the town, the piled sandbags outside the council house and the town hall appeared to be higher than ever.

During the day — so we heard later — Neville Chamberlain told his cabinet that the event which the government had fought so long and so earnestly to avoid had now come upon them. "But" he added, "our consciences are clear, and there should be no possible question now where our duties lie". Britain sent an ultimatum to Germany, demanding that she should withdraw her troops from Poland, and the tension increased. On Saturday there was general mobilisation, bringing in its wake a spate of proclamations for calling up the Navy, the Army and the Air Force reserves, embodying the Territorial Army, and other matter preceding a declaration of war. A million children were evacuated from what were termed 'vulnerable areas' of the country.

The fateful hour was to be eleven o'clock, British Summer Time, on Sunday morning, 3rd September, when the British ultimatum expired. I was up early that morning, mooning around and somewhat restless, when I met Douglas from across the road, (there were three of us Douglases living within a few yards of each other). We chatted about the days ahead. "It's the R.A.F. and flying for me!" said Douglas. I wasn't surprised to hear it, for he was mad about 'planes and flying, and spent every moment he could spare down at Castle Bromwich Aerodrome, the home of 605 Squadron, R.A.F.

We knew that the Prime Minister was speaking on the wireless at 11.15 and Douglas came into my home where, with my mother and father, we tuned in for that time and listened to the chastened voice of Chamberlain as he addressed the nation:

> *"I am speaking to you from the cabinet*
> *room at 10, Downing Street. This morning*
> *the British Ambassador in Berlin handed*
> *the German government a final note,*
> *stating that unless we heard from them by*

*11 o'clock that they were prepared
at once to withdraw their troops from
Poland, a state of war would exist
between us. I have to tell you now
that no such undertaking has been
received, and that consequently this
country is at war with Germany . . . ."*

Poor Douglas! It was a death-sentence for him. He was turned down for flying duties on medical grounds, joined the Royal Tank Regiment and, two years later, was killed in a tank in the Western Desert.

*   *   *   *   *

Within minutes of Chamberlain's broadcast, air-raid sirens sounded in London, 'buses and trains stopped, and people ran for shelter. But nothing drastic happened, either then or in the days ahead, and the populace adjusted to the state of quiescence, soon to be dubbed the 'phoney war' or the 'great bore war'. Most of the early war-time casualties were due to accidents in the black-out, which plunged the whole country into inky blackness on every moonless night. Any use of torch or matches, however momentary, usually resulted in an air raid warden looming out of the void to give voice to his new-found authority.

At Sutton Coldfield there was a Balloon Barrage Depot, and we soon became accustomed to the sight of those silver, hydrogen-filled balloons, glistening in the September sky. Their purpose, we were told, was to reduce the likelihood of low-level air attacks or dive-bombing, but no-one seemed to know if they were effective in the role for which they were designed, or if their gentle and amiable presence overhead was merely a ploy on the part of the authorities to bolster up the morale of the people. The balloons over London certainly acted as an antidote to the prevailing jitteriness, induced by the forecast of horrible happenings on the Home Front accompanying the outbreak of war. The populace had been led to believe that 'instant annihilation' from the air was to be expected, and one scientist of the day — J.B.S. Haldane — had predicted that the opening German air-attack on

*Sending up a
barrage balloon, 1939*

London might kill between 50,000 and 100,000 of its citizens. But all
remained quiet.

A British Expeditionary Force of four divisions was sent to France,
and plans were formulated by the cabinet for the eventual creation of a
fifty-five division army, but the whole front — protected on the German
side by the Siegfried Line and on the French side by the Maginot Line
— remained in a state of passivity. During the first three months of the
war, in which Germany proceeded to destroy the Polish army in the
field, not a single British soldier was killed on the Western Front. The
R.A.F. contented itself with dropping propaganda leaflets on Germany,
and the only arm of the services to be engaged in anything like active

BIRMINGHAM CALM

LORD MAYOR'S CALL TO CITIZENS

"THE TESTING TIME HAS COME"

PROGRESS OF CITY'S DEFENCES

The people of Birmingham and the Midlands enter upon the war with calm resolve and determination. There is neither fear nor flag-wagging. From all the organisations which are appealing for help comes news of a steady and gratifying response.

The Lord Mayor has issued the following message to citizens:—

The testing time has come, and I am confident that the citizens of Birmingham will meet it with determination and calmness.

I earnestly hope that all citizens will give careful attention to the directions given for their safety over the wireless and through press notices, and that they will strictly obey the instructions.

The work of protecting important buildings in the city nears completion; while new measures for the safety of the public in the provision of air raid shelters, and for coping with any damage to property or injury to citizens are increasing. Day and night vigilant watch is kept to detect approaching danger.

During Friday and Saturday 40,000 people were evacuated from the city, 30,000 school-children under the official scheme, and mothers with young children, expectant mothers and aged and infirm people. Arrangements had been made to send away 70,000 schoolchildren, but the number was reduced by absences on family holidays and by the ultimate reluctance of mothers to let their children go before an emergency was upon us.

Many now wish to send their children away. Unless ordered by the Government, no official arrangements can be made at present. Parents who will arrange the journey personally may get information at the Education Offices, Margaret Street.

The Auxiliary Fire Service, under Mr. S. H. Johnson, is declared to be in a fully organised state. Mr. Johnson has expressed his appreciation of the magnificent work performed with enthusiasm at all hours, by officers and men to prepare for emergencies.

Women with experience of clerical and telephone work are needed for day and night service. Application should be made at Fire Brigade headquarters.

Volunteers are needed for rescue and clearance service. They should have experience of building trade work, be not less than 30, and physically fit. Applications should be made to Public Works depots.

Mr. John Howell, City A.R.P. Transport Officer, appeals to all motorists who have enrolled but not yet reported to do so at once. Other volunteers are needed.

About 40 recruits are needed in the Business Men's Squadron of the Birmingham Balloon Barrage, South Centre, age 30-50. Application at Squadron Office, Wythall, 10 a.m. to 6 p.m.

Food Committee

At a meeting of Birmingham General Purposes Committee to-day the following members of the Food Committee were appointed:—The Lord Mayor and Alderman Sir Ernest Canning, Councillors Mrs. Clarke, Miss Kenrick, Councillors A. F. Bradbeer, W. H. Griss, —. Potts, H. Richardson, A. H. Cooper and J. N. Spalton.

Trade members appointed are Messrs. T. G. Arnold, grocer and provision merchant, of 210-211, Monument Road. Edgbaston; E. Burton, retail butcher, of 106, Lichfield Road, Aston; J. W. Fletcher, of Birmingham Co-operative Society. High Street; Councillor A. W. Gurden, of Wathes Cattell and Gurden, Ltd., Nova Scotia Street; and E. Harding, of the Royal Steam Bakery, Yardley.

Mr. J. P. Eames, deputy City Treasurer, is the Executive Food Officer. Sir James Curtis is the Divisional Food Officer.

Food supplies will be secured by the householders in the normal manner for the moment—but only in normal quantities. Excessive buying is now a crime, and seller and purchaser responsible for it would be liable to severe punishment. Ration cards will be issued in due course.

Birmingham remains calm in the crisis.
An extract from the "Birmingham Mail" of 4th September 1939.

service was the Royal Navy. Winston Churchill described the period as 'a prolonged and oppressive pause', and the British people were puzzled by what seemed to them to be the non-event of all time.

* * * * *

Familiar faces disappeared from among one's friends and acquaintances, sometimes to reappear at week-ends, re-attired in uniforms which, if not always a good fit, imparted a certain glamour to their wearers in the eyes of local girls. By and large, however, there was nothing comparable with the great rush to the colours at the outbreak of war in 1914, and conscription was already on the statute books. My own dilemma was a common enough one. Should I wait for the call-up or should I exercise some very small measure of choice over how I was to spend the days ahead? Despite a long-standing distaste for war, nurtured by my mentors since early childhood, the only feasible alternative — conscientious objection — did not appeal to me in the light of events, and I decided to choose an arm of the service for myself, with some help from my family and friends. After numerous discussions with Ernie Bowater, Vic Cox — who was taking the plunge with me — and others, I decided to join the Royal Engineers. This was a decision based partly on a promise by a recruiting sergeant that if Vic and I enlisted together in that Corps we would be able to serve together for the duration of the war — a promise which proved to be quite specious for, having acted on his advice, we were separated within a few weeks, and our paths did not cross again for six years.

Before joining up I went to see Mr. Jerromes to ask his permission to do so and to ensure that the council would make up the difference between my meagre two shillings (10p) a day army pay and my salary of £105 a year. Mr. Jerromes, who had been an officer in the 1914 — 1918 war, showed an unexpected degree of warmth and charm, and having given permission for my departure, together with an assurance that my job would be awaiting me on my return, added his blessings and good wishes for the future. Within a month of war breaking out, Vic and I had completed the formalities, passed our medicals with flying colours and taken the 'King's Shilling' after having been sworn in. We were also issued with railway warrants, authorising our journey to Chatham, where we were to report to the ominously named

1881206 Sapper D.V. Jones, R.E.

Kitchener Barracks, and on a calm autumn morning at the beginning of October, 1939, we set out on the first leg of our war-time travels.

A new world was about to break over the horizon: a world of blanco, button-sticks, rifle-drill, roll-calls, church parades, kit inspections, guard duties, square-bashing, firing on the range, mine-laying, pontoon bridging over swirling rivers on moon-less nights, demolitions, map-reading and knots and lashes. It was a world, too, of menial tasks: potato-peeling, dish-washing, coal-heaving, snow-shifting and man-handling heavy engineering stores, together with a broad spectrum of seemingly completely useless activities, involving much stamping, strutting and posturing on the parade-ground — all done by numbers — and encapsulated in a much-used military phrase: 'Bull-shit baffles brains!'

I had become 'Sapper D.V. Jones, R.E. No. 1881206', answering henceforward to the stentorian call to duty: 'Jones, '206!'

*   *   *   *   *

Bygone Birmingham

A pictorial supplement to chapter V

Photographs reproduced by courtesy of Birmingham Public Library, Local
Studies Department

A B Row, showing the old parish boundary-stone marking the boundary
between the parishes of Aston and Birmingham which gave the thoroughfare its name. Aston was once a place of considerable size and at the time
of the Domesday Survey it was more important than Birmingham

Broad Street site of the Hall of Memory in 1922

Opening of the Hall of Memory in July, 1925

High Street, Birmingham, c. 1925

Corporation Street in 1927

Lichfield Road, Aston, 1921

And the same place in 1930, showing the dual carriageway

Kingstanding Road in April, 1928
Birmingham during the inter-war years was expanding into the countryside around its perimeter

Marks and Spencer's Stores in High Street, Birmingham, c. 1930,
destroyed by incendiary bombs in 1941

Corporation Street, c. 1930

A Birmingham car park, October, 1931

The Minories, looking towards the Old Square, February, 1932

Victoria Square in 1932

Steam scene, New Street Station, date unknown

The 'Fox and Goose' and the Washwood Heath tram terminus,
September, 1933

End of the day exodus from the Austin Motor Company's Works at
Longbridge, c. 1935

Deritend, junction of Rea Street, May, 1934

St. John's Church, Deritend, c. 1935, demolished for road widening in 1947

Clock in Dale End Arcade,
later moved to the Market Hall,
where it was destroyed
during World War II

Interior of Birmingham Market Hall, June, 1936, destroyed by enemy
action during World War II

Broad Street, showing the now demolished Unitarian Church, May, 1936

New Street, decorated for the Coronation of King George VI in 1937

Lancaster Place, February, 1932

And the same spot in September, 1937, showing the Central Fire Station

St. Martin's Lane, looking towards Edgbaston Street, 1935

Edmund Street, c.1937

The Bull Ring and St. Martin's Church in 1937

The Old Crown Inn, Deritend, 1937

The junction of Jamaica Row and Edgbaston Street, 23rd March, 1938

A 'trial run' for Egbert, the dragon, who featured in the pageant of 1938, commemorating the centenary of Birmingham's Charter of Incorporation in that year

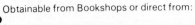

Westwood Press Publications

THE ROYAL TOWN of SUTTON COLDFIELD
A Commemorative History
by Douglas V. Jones

A warm human story of local people, events and landmarks written in an easy style that holds the reader's interest from first to last page.

208 pages fully illustrated and including: A SPECIAL INSET MAP circa 1800

Standard Edition Limp Cover   **Price £4.95** (post/packing 80p)

Collectors Hardback Edition with gold blocked cloth cover signed personally by the Author   **Price £9.50** (post/packing £1.10)

SUTTON PARK Its History and Wildlife
by Douglas V. Jones

Profusely illustrated with a wide selection of old and new pictures most of which have not previously been published. Complete with inset map and three interesting walks.   **Price £0.00** (post/packing 30p)

SUTTON COLDFIELD 1974-1984 The Story of a Decade
by Douglas V. Jones

A lavishly illustrated Chronicle which recalls the many changes to the face of Sutton since its merger with Birmingham ten years ago, together with a Pictorial Supplement, *Sutton in 1984*. A record of the events and issues which have evoked public interest, concern, sympathy and other mixed emotions during the decade, this short book is an up-dating of the story of a town with a proud and ancient past.

Price £2.50 (post/packing 35p)

STEAMING UP TO SUTTON How the Birmingham to Sutton Coldfield Railway Line was built in 1862
written by Roger Lea

Every day thousands travel on the railway line between Sutton and Birmingham, without giving much thought to its origins and history. From Duddeston to Aston their journey is on the route of the first trunk railway in the world, the Grand Junction, but this book is concerned with the humbler origins of the five miles from Aston to Sutton. What happened in the twenty-five years between the opening of the Grand Junction in 1837 and the Sutton Branch in 1862? Why choose this particular route rather than others proposed? What were the hopes and fears of its promoters and opponents?   **Price £2.25** (post/packing 35p)

. . . continued overleaf

Westwood Press Publications

THE BOOK OF BRUM or 'Mekya Selfa Tum'   by Ray Tennant

Random thoughts on the dialect and accent of the Second City (Brumslang) with a glossary of the most common expressions plus Brumodes, Brumverse and Brumericks with a little more serious verse.   **Price £1.50** (post/packing 30p)

AWARE DIN UREA A Second Book of Brum   by Ray Tennant

Further thoughts on the dialect and accent of Birmingham with a glossary containing many sayings of historical interest plus a little more verse and cartoons by Lyndon. Many expressions from the past are included in this Second Book of Brum.   **Price £1.95** (post/packing 30p)

SOLID CITIZENS Statues in Birmingham   by Bridget Pugh
with drawings by Anne Irby Crews

Presenting a collection of illustrations and accounts of some of the main figures to be found in the city. Together they represent the history of Birmingham and those associated with it during the last thousand years.   **Price £1.95** (post/packing 30p)

LAST TRAM DOWN THE VILLAGE And Other Memories of Yesterday's Birmingham   by Ray Tennant

This is a book about journeys of two kinds. The first are normal ones concerned with travel from place to place and the memories evoked from arriving. But it is also about journeys in time, journeys in the mind which again bring back memories.

Although all the places written about are centred in or very near to Birmingham it will, hopefully, be of interest to people who live in other cities since many of the memories could be shared and appreciated by anyone who lived through the traumatic years of the thirties and forties . . . someone once called nostalgia 'A Pleasant Kind of Ache' which is a very apt description!   **Price £2.95**
(post/packing 35p)

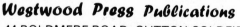 Obtainable from Bookshops or direct from:

Westwood Press Publications
44 BOLDMERE ROAD, SUTTON COLDFIELD
* When ordering by post please add Postage as marked
Three books ordered together Postfree